Abu Dhabi's Old Is Gold!

Urban Planning Memories

By

Assad El Abbas

Table of Contents

Dedication i

Acknowledgement iii

Introduction 1

Historical Background 4

Chapter 1: H.H Sheikh Zayed The UAE Founder 20

Sheikh Zayed's Profile: 20

Zayed The Beloved Personality: 22

Zayed the Green Hands: 24

Zayed The UAE Founder: 30

Zayed and Education: 31

Zayed's Dreams Come True: 33

Chapter 2: Al Nahyan Shoulder To Shoulder (1928- Now) 35

Chapter 3: Abu Dhabi Culture 40

Trust, Honesty, Generosity: 40

Camel the Desert's Ship: 41

UAE Heritage: 44

The Burjeel: 45

The Ruler's Hand Stick: 47

Diving (Al Ghous): 49

Al Yasat Community (Al Fareej): 51

Chapter 4: Abu Dhabi Old Days 56

Sas Al Nakhl Archaeology: 56

The Trucial States before Oil: 57

Al Maqta Crossing Way: 59

Al Maqta Metalwork Bridge: 60

Abu Dhabi Year to Year Calender: 63

Chapter 5: Abu Dhabi Oil Exploration 69

ADPC (Abu Dhabi Petroleum Company): 69

ADPC's Survey Teams: 71

Oil and Gas in Abu Dhabi: 73

ADMA - Opco: 75

Chapter 6: Abu Dhabi Top 5 Departments 79

Department of Abu Dhabi Municipality: 79

Department of Planning & Coordination: 95

Department of Information and Tourism: 96

Department of Civil Aviation: 98

Department of Public Works: 101

Chapter 7: On The Desert's Dunes 108

Wilfred Thesiger: 108

Edward Henderson: 109

Hugh Boustead: 110

William Halcrow: 111

John Harris: 112

Tim & Suzan Hillyard: 112

Roderic Owen: 114

Wanda Jablonski: 116

William Round (The Old Brit): 118

Nick Choshrane (Mankabi): 120

Chapter 8: Earlier British Activities In The Trucial States.................. 122

First Coastal Survey of Trucial States: 122

British Political Agency: 123

National Agents: 124

The Saint Joseph's Church: 125

British Consultants and Contractors in the Trucial States (Samples only): 126

Chapter 9: Early Arrivals In Abu Dhabi 128

Victor Hashim: 128

Emil Al Busstani: 129

Dr. Sayed Kurayem: 129

Dr. Abdulrahman Makhlouf: 132

Al Sunny Banaga: 133

Ahmed Awad Al Karim: 135

Dr. Omer Al Khatib: 136

Hanna Elias Khraish: 137

Mohammed Mandi: 140

Joseph Dally 142

Radwan Al Tamimi (Abu Tafish): 143

Chapter 10: Abu Dhabi Amazing Architecture 146

Octagonal Building, Abu Dhabi Corniche: 146

ADMA Office Building: 147

Mohamed Harib Al Otaiba Building: 148

ADNOC Residential Complex: 149

Al Omeira Building: 150

Al Kalily Building: 151

Mariam Bint Sultan Building: 152

Hamed Center: 153

Cultural Foundation: 154

Chapter 11: Abu Dhabi Top 5 Mosques 155

Zayed Bin Sultan Al-Nahyan Mosque: 155

Zayed the 1st Grand Mosque: 164

Sheikh Sultan Bin Zayed The First Mosque: 165

Khalifa Bin Zayed The 1st Mosque: 167

Mariam Um Eisa Mosque (PBUT): 169

Chapter 12: Abu Dhabi Top 5 Palaces 171

Qasr Al Hosn: 171

Qasr Al Manhal: 174

Qasr Al Mushref: 175

Qasr Al Bahr: 177

Qasr Al Watan: 178

Chapter 13: Abu Dhabi Top 5 Oldest Markets (Souks)...................... 180

Arabicon Central Market: 180

Old Central Market: 181

New Central Market:..183

Vegetables, Meat, Fish & Clothes Market (W2): 185

Madinat Zayed Shopping Center: 188

Chapter 14: Abu Dhabi Top 5 Oldest Hotels............................... 190

Subhan Allah Hotel:..190

The Beach Hotel: 192

Khalidiya Palace Hotel: 194

Al-Ain Palace Hotel: 196

Abu Dhabi Hilton Hotel:..198

Chapter 15: Abu Dhabi Top 5 Oldest Cinemas 200

BP's – Cinema: 200

Al Maria Cinema: 201

Al Ferdous Cinema: 203

The National Cinema: 204

Eldorado Cinema: 205

Chapter 16: Abu Dhabi Top 5 Oldest Clubs................................ 207

The Club: 207

Al Emarat Sports Club: 210

The Police Club: 213

Abu Dhabi Sports Club: 214

Tourist Club: 216

Chapter 17: Abu Dhabi Top 5 Old Hospitals............................... 219

The Central Hospital: 219

Al Jazeera Hospital: 220

Corniche Hospital: 222

Mafraq Hospital: 225

Zayed Military Hospital: 226

Chapter 18: Abu Dhabi Top 5 Oldest Cemeteries 228

Al Bateen Cemetery: 228

Al Dana 3 Cemetery: 229

Zayed City Cemetery 1: 230

Corniche Cemetery: 231

Um Al Nar (Sas Al Nakhl Non Muslim Cemetry): 232

Chapter 19: Abu Dhabi Top 5 Oldest Parks 234

Al Khalidiya Park: 234

Al Asima Park: 235

Family Park: 237

Old Airport Park: 238

Um Al Emarat Park: 239

Chapter 20: Top 5 Demolished But Still Remembered 241

Old Custom House: 241

Clock Tower: 243

Volcano Fountain: 244

GCC Fountain: 245

.... 246

Al Hosn Mosque: 246

Chapter 21: Author's Top 5 Artwork Designs 249

UAE University Logo: 249

UAE 15th National Day Stamp Design: 250

Al Jazeera Club Logo Design: 250

UNICEF Stamp Designs 251

Safe Energy Stamps: 252

Chapter 22: Miscellaneous 254

Cloth Washing (Dhobi Ghat): 254

Lilam: 255

Old Taxi Service: 256

Randomly 80s-90s Shop Names: 257

Chapter 23: Questionnaire 260

Q&A...260

About The Author 272

Book References 274

Dedication

This memorial book, *ABU DHABI'S OLD IS GOLD! Urban Planning Memories* is dedicated to the Soul of His Highness Sheikh Zayed Bin Sultan Al Nahyan (1918-2004), the President of the United Arab Emirates (1971-2004).

Although H.H Sheikh Zayed is the Founder of the United Arab Emirates, his successor the Pedident H.H Sheikh Khalifa Bin Zayed and His Crown Prince H.H Sheikh Mohammed Bin Zayed played important roles in developing Abu Dhabi City from a fishermen's town into a splendid capital city inhabiting almost two millions of inhabitants, and welcoming millions of visitors year by year.

H.H Sheikh Zayed (RIP), passed away with great regret on 2nd November, 2004, but H.H. is always in mind being the actual town planner of Abu Dhabi City.

Acknowledgement

Each of us has a nice place that embraced his dreams. That place embarked a lot of joy and happiness. When we leave that beloved place, we close our eyes and glance at it with our imagination and hold it in our hearts.

The images of buildings, neighbours and friends at that beloved place are always remembered. Also the streets where our family house was located, the market we used to go for shopping, and the school locations and classmates in mind. Always one realizes that nothing was more beautiful and closer to the heart than that place where we lived our beautiful old good days.

First of all I wish to thank each and every one encouraged me to share the information and my memories I have as an eye witness in Abu Dhabi Town Planning for almost 44 years of continuous service in Abu Dhabi Municipality (1968-2012).

Special thanks to my close friends and directors, the Late Mr. Takahashi Abu Dhabi Chief Town Planner (1967-1968), and thanks extended to Dr Abdelrahman Makhlouf who has been my godfather and shared together our dreams, photos, maps, and text information. I do appreciate his writings and wonderful memories of Abu Dhabi City and his book (Rehlat Al Omr Ma Al Omran). May his soul rest in peace.

Special thanks to all my TPD family members, especially Eng. Samy El Dasher, Head of Planning Section and all my soulmate honestly worked together. Also Mr. Mustafa Al Musawa of TPS Spatial Data Directorate, and nowadays Smart Navigation Pioneer.

Finally, I am in debt to those lovely friends of (Abu Dhabi Good Old Days) Group members especially Mr. Paul Woodlock who enriched my mind by sharing their day to day memories. Also those unknown media soldiers and live correspondents and editors who stand on the events' frontline, especially Al Ittihad, Al Bayan , Gulf News, Emirates Today (Al Emarat Al Youm), and The National Newspapers, for their detailed coverage. Also to those pioneers of Abu Dhabi early days, whether they are UAE nationals or expatriates who spent their lives working hard on site or inside their offices, and offered every effort to develop Abu Dhabi City to be such a wonderful place to live in.

Introduction

H.H Sheikh Zayed Bin Sultan Al Nahyan UAE Founder RIP, H.H Sheikh Khalifa Bin Zayed Al Nahyan UAE President, H.H Sheikh Mohammed Bin Zayed Al Nahyan Crown Prince, ADE De Facto Ruler.

To write about Abu Dhabi City is to write about the UAE, and to write about the UAE is to write about the leader His Highness Sheikh Zayed Bin Sultan Al Nahyan, His successor H.H Sheikh Khalifa bin Zayed, and His Crown Prince, His Highness Sheikh Mohammed bin Zayed Al-Nahyan.

Zayed is the Founder of the UAE and the talented Town Planner of its beautiful capital Abu Dhabi, as well as the garden cities of Abu Dhabi Emirate.

Since H.H became the Ruler of Abu Dhabi Emirate, on August 6th 1966, His Highness Sheikh Zayed Bin Sultan Al-Nahyan has lead the ship of development to transfer the UAE from darkness to lightness, from poverty to wealth, and from isolation to openness. He moved the country from a desolate unknown Trucial States to a prosperous well known United Arab Emirates with its bright future.

In the last five decades of the UAE, many things have been changed and the towns of the UAE had become major cities in every meaning of the word. Abu Dhabi became the capital city. A huge construction movement that covered the desert and hugged the sky with its skyscrapers, tower buildings, and projects taking the mind. All this was to build a homeland full of happiness for both deprived UAE citizens and expatriates arrived from different parts of the world.

The UAE has become a modern country referred to, and its capital, Abu Dhabi, has become a tourism destination, home of charm and beauty, and the place of local and international exhibitions. Besides that, human creativities and aspirations for the future have been evolved in the UAE.

It was a comprehensive urban development in various fields lead by his successors, with determination: Mosques, schools, universities, public houses, residential villas, iconic buildings, gardens, stadiums and sports clubs were built. Hospitals, health centers, social care homes, women's associations, marriage fund, loans, social services, electricity, water, communications networks, markets, banks, charities, shopping malls, ports, airports, factories, roads and bridges, pedestrian tunnels, police and security headquarters and control stations. All this was done so that everyone can enjoy freedom, security, happiness and independence.

The guidance of His Highness the Father RIP, and following up the projects by himself in the stages of planning and implementation have had a great impact and the main reason that the cities become in such a splendor. Abu Dhabi city to won the first rank in environmental safety in the Arab countries, and won many international awards in the years after.

Abu Dhabi visitors are amazed and the residents enjoys a well-off life and enjoy luxurious residences, beautiful gardens and picturesque beaches. The fingerprints of His Highness Sheikh Zayed Bin Sultan Al-Nahyan, His successor, His Highness Sheikh Khalifa Bin Zayed Al Nahyan, and His Crown Prince, H.H Sheikh Mohammed Bin Zayed Al Nahyan are visible in every part of our beloved country.

Historical Background

The first thing that interests us when studying the formation of Abu Dhabi city and its urbanisation is its site selection and the factors that influenced and affected its geographical and urban location.

Abu Dhabi Emirate is located on the Arabian Gulf between latitudes 22°40' and around 25° North and longitudes 51° and around 56° East, with an area of 67,340 km2, equivalent to 86.7% of the UAE total area. Abu Dhabi is a very less populated Emirate.

The Emirate of Abu Dhabi consists of three municipal areas:

1. The first is Abu Dhabi City Area, which is located on the island of Abu Dhabi and the surrounding areas, including the villages on Abu Dhabi-Al Ain, Abu Dhabi-Dubai, and Abu Dhabi-Al Dhafra highways.

2. The second is Al Ain area, which was known as the Eastern Region in the past.

3. The third is Al-Dhafra area, which includes Madinat Zayed and Liwa, was known as the Western Region, where most of the oil and gas fields, and refineries are located.

Abu Dhabi Municipal Divisions/ TPS

Abu Dhabi city is the federal capital of the United Arab Emirates, where the Presidency Dewan, the Council of Ministers and Embassies exist. It is the centre of government activities, the World Trade Center and the business hub. The city has gone through many stages of development, becoming in a short time a modern international city, characterised by its distinctive architectural designs and modernity: wide clean streets, amazing gardens, beautiful corniche, and beaches.

The most important part of Abu Dhabi city is located on Abu Dhabi Island, connected to the mainland by four stunning bridges.

Here is a brief history of the city's development: Abu Dhabi Town construction is a commutative process passed historically through 6 distinctive stages according to my analysis:

1.   **The site choosing** of Abu Dhabi town was in 1761. It had been historically chosen for security, social and economic purposes, keeping in mind the city will be the capital of Abu Dhabi Emirate instead of Al Maria in Liwa Oasis. The town was randomly developed during the decades before the discovery of oil in 1958.

Al Dhahr was the top portion of Abu Dhabi Island where the old town and the small jetty (Al Fardha) was formulated.

Al Bateen is located near Khor Al Bateen. The old Al Bateen village consisted, like Al Dhahr, of palm fronds, huts and cottages.

The earlier inhabitants of Al-Bateen were from Al Suweidan and Al Bumhair tribes who were engaged in diving, shipbuilding, and fishing.

Simplicity, compassion and generosity were and still the distinctive qualities of the people of Abu Dhabi. Abu Dhabi Island's population were few, and all inhabitants knew each other. Life was difficult due to the lack of money, and workers were receiving their salaries in Indian Rubees and later in Bahraini dinars, the prevailing currency in Abu Dhabi, while the currency in the Northern Emirates was the Dubai and Qatari riyal.

2. **The preliminary stage,** which was commissioned by H.H Sheikh Shakhbout (RIP). By choosing Sir William Halcrow and Scott Wilson Kirk Patrick & Partners, to submit a field survey report and to prepare a structural plan for the city of Abu Dhabi in February 1962.

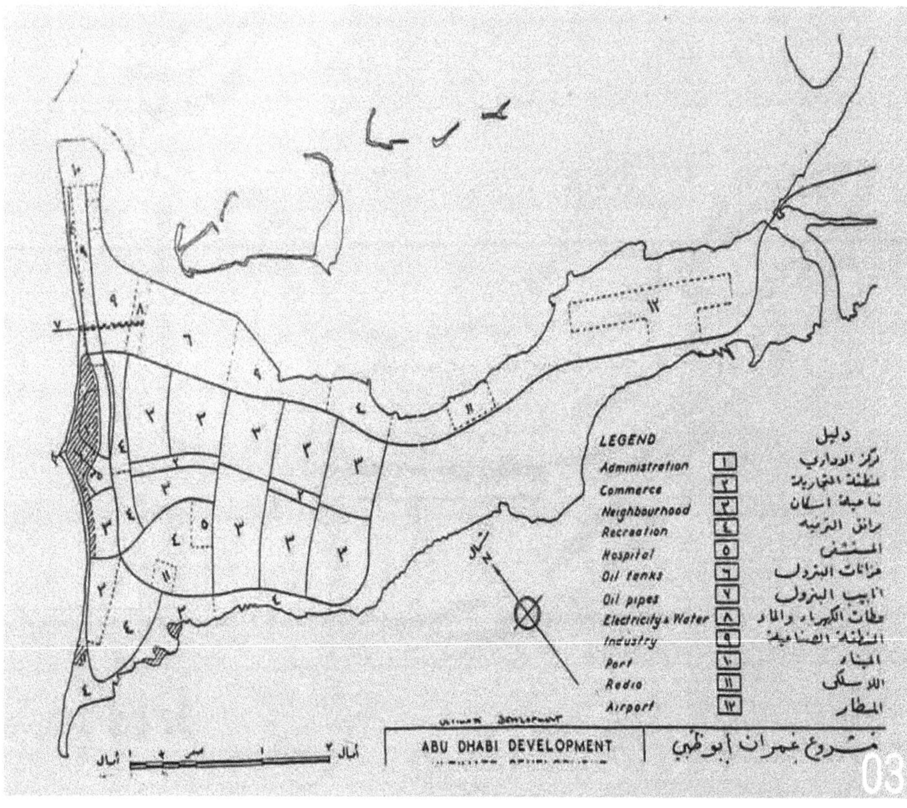

This process was supervised by the Late Hugh Boustead, the British Agent (1961-1965). The later tried to adopt the Plan of Morocco, capital city, Al Rabat, which was welcomed by Sheikh Shakhbout. Mr. Boustead wrote to the British Agent in Morocco to supply him with drawings and photos of Al Rabat City for this purpose.

In 1965, Sheikh Shakhbout (RIP) signed an agreement with Arabicon Consultants. Arabicon was selected by the Ruler as the Architectural consultants to carry out a range of works, including the construction of Abu Dhabi Fardha (Jetty), internal main streets, and Abu Dhabi-Al Ain Road. (*info: Fatima M. Al Mansouri, ADHC*)

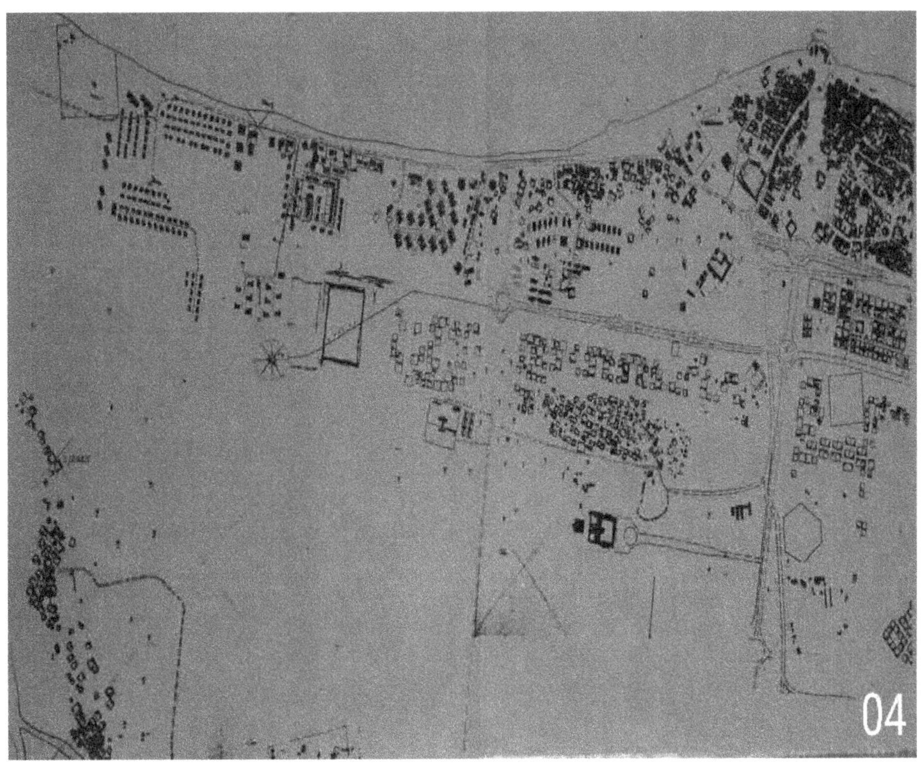

Map Source: TPD

In February 1966, Sheikh Shakhbout instructed Messrs Arabicon to carry out Town Planning tasks and implement three basic projects linking Abu Dhabi to the world: Abu Dhabi Airport, Al Maqta bridge, and Harbour.

Arabicon was a British Company founded in Abu Dhabi by Messrs. Alan Grant and Associates/ Surry England/ Eddie Webb/ and Ian Cuthbert. The latter has been appointed as the company's interim representative in Abu Dhabi.

3.   City Transitional stage, Arabicon Takhashi 1966-1968:

This was when Halcrow design was revised by His Highness Sheikh Zayed and Arabicon, ordered to modify the plan into the grid network. Thus, straight roads have been adopted.

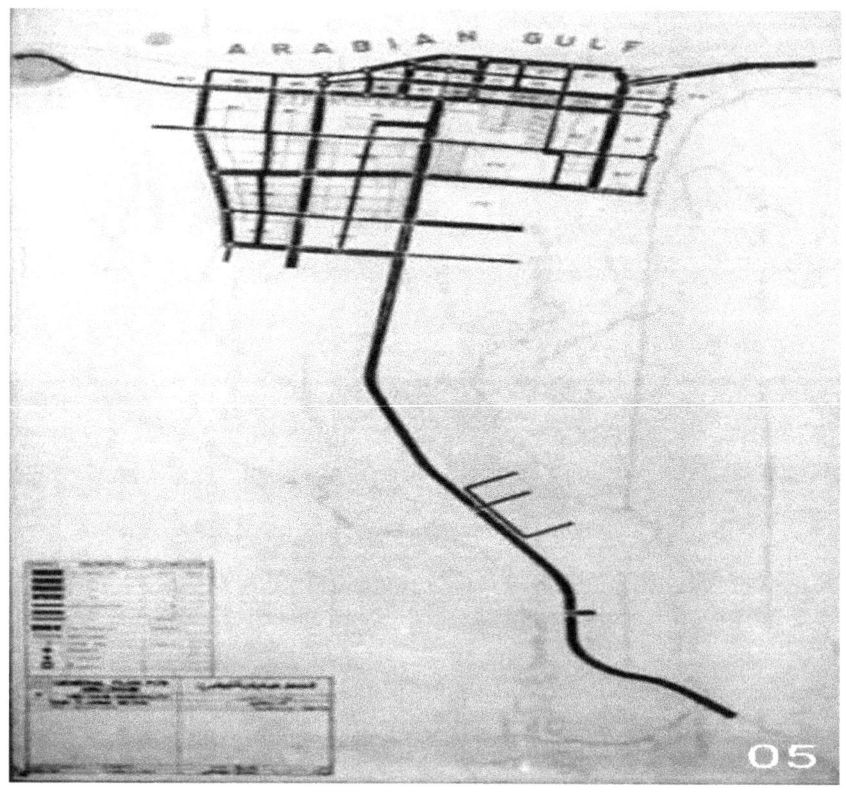

Photo Source: Planning Abu Dhabi, an Urban History/ Alamira Reem Bani Hashim Book

Architect Katsuhiko Takahashi, Chief Town Planner. Source: (TPS)

His Highness, Sheikh Zayed bin Sultan Al Nahyan as ruler of Abu Dhabi, appointed the Japanese UN Town Planner, Mr. Takahashi, to supervise the plan's implementation in 1967.

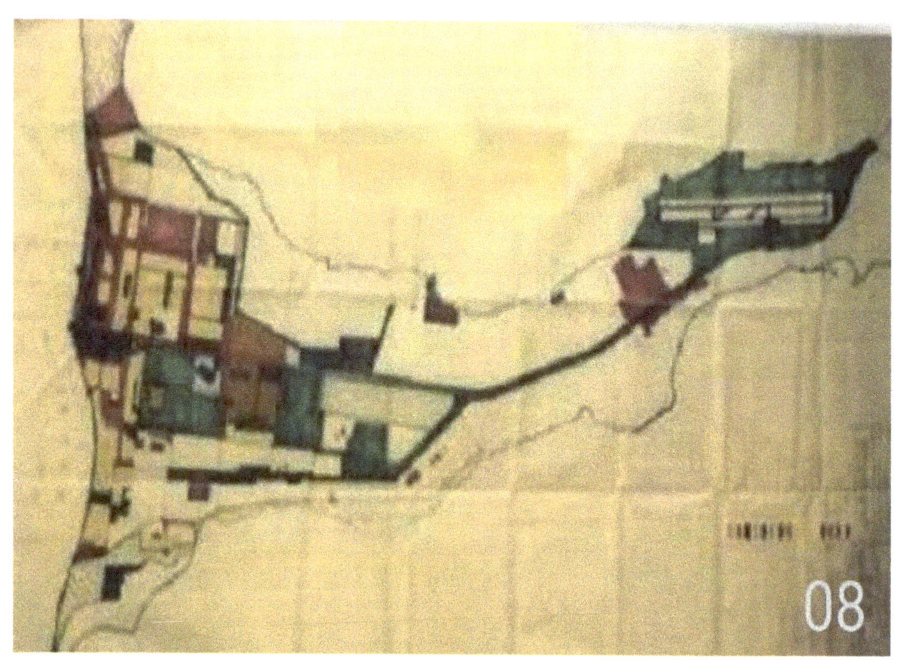

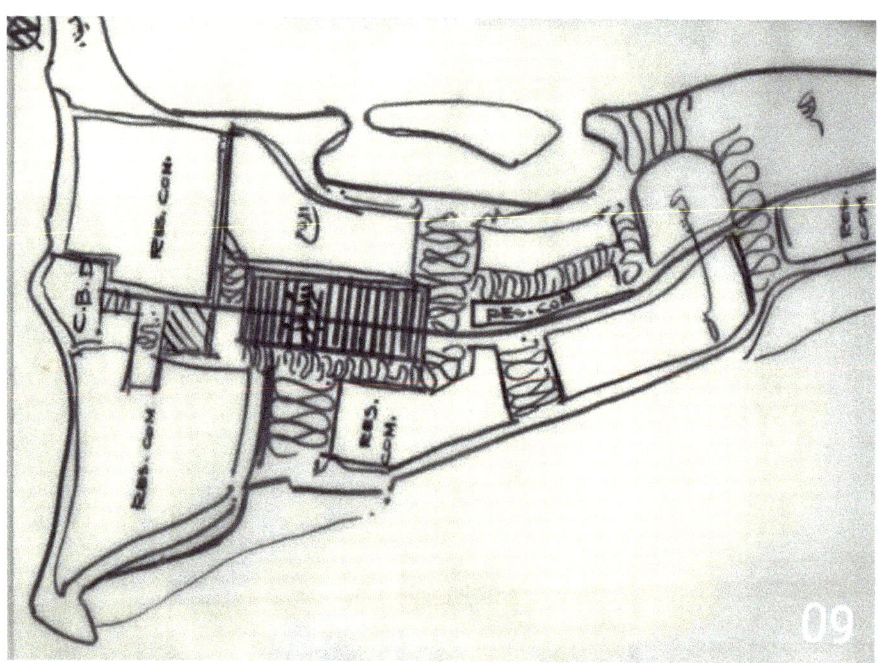

Source: TPD/ self-drawn and coloured

4.   The stage of Town Planning Department organised planning under full governmental supervision (1968-1976).

In the year 1968, His Highness Sheikh Zayed bin Sultan Al Nahyan has appointed Dr. Abdulrahman Makhlouf, the formerly UN urban planning expert in Saudi Arabia, as director of Town Planning in the emirate of Abu Dhabi.

Dr Makhlouf demonstrating CBD 1969. Source: (Dr Makhlouf)

Dr. Makhlouf has developed Abu Dhabi Master Plan, and detailed plans for the city's Eastern and Western sectors determined the land use and the population densities of the areas according to those uses and managed the implementation of the Master Plans of Abu Dhabi city, Al Ain, Madinat Zayed, and the villages located on the roads leading to them. He also managed the implementation of several housing projects, major roads, central markets, public buildings, and service projects. Dr. Makhlouf is considered to be a professional town planner and architect.

The Central Area was the main core of the city, where old buildings were completely removed except Qasr Al Hosn. CBD was determined in 1968 on the basis of density 150 people/acre.

The central area underwent some modifications in 1973 by abolishing commercial plots in Sector E8 and W7/02 by allocating E8 to be the Al Asima Park and W7/02 to be the Corniche Garden (Family Park).

The area expanded between 1978 and 1983. Residential areas adjacent to the central area have been re-planned to become low-rise buildings.

It was the most beautiful day of my life, on the morning of 2nd December 1971, when I saw the flags of the UAE flapping on the electric poles and everywhere. The UAE hands had turned into one hand, and the era of deprivation has been washed away. The country has opened its doors to Arab and foreign experiences and workers from various parts of the world.

As soon as he completed his duties as director of the Town Planning Department in 1976, Dr. Makhlouf established the Arab Office for Planning and Architecture to complete his role and satisfy his passion for serving the UAE that we love. I had the pleasure of accompanying hcomplete1968 to 1976.

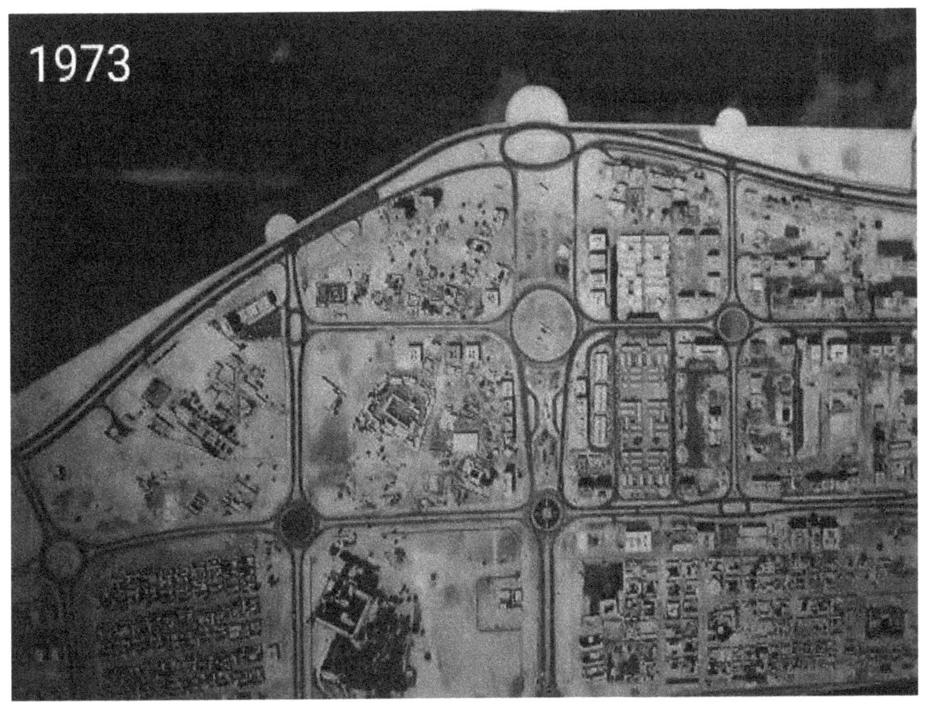

5.   The stage of horizontal and vertical development (1976-2007): which witnessed the appointment of Engineer Azmi Abu Taleb as director of Town Planning Department where the Abu Dhabi Government appointed Messrs Deluew Cather International for the Project to improve roads and traffic signals (Trip Project) in 1979 and Messers W.S. Atkins & Partners Overseas were appointed as consultants to prepare the development master plan for greater Abu Dhabi in 1990.

Upgrading commercial buildings to more number of floors and higher levels were allowed by the Building License Section of Abu Dhabi Town

Planning Department, in collaboration with the Department of Social Services and Commercial Buildings in 1982, to meet the requirements of the vertical extension of the commercial buildings. The necessary government funding with full supervision of the project and the task of managing and supervising the buildings the banks held was transferred to the Department of Social Services and Commercial Buildings up to 2006.

Demolishing as easy work was going on Liwa Street (Lulu Street now) in 1988. New towers like the one shown in Black / White horizontally stripped on the right of the photo is Sheikh Hamid Tower, where Emirates Islamic Bank took its office on the Corniche Road.

Photo Source: Assad El Abbas

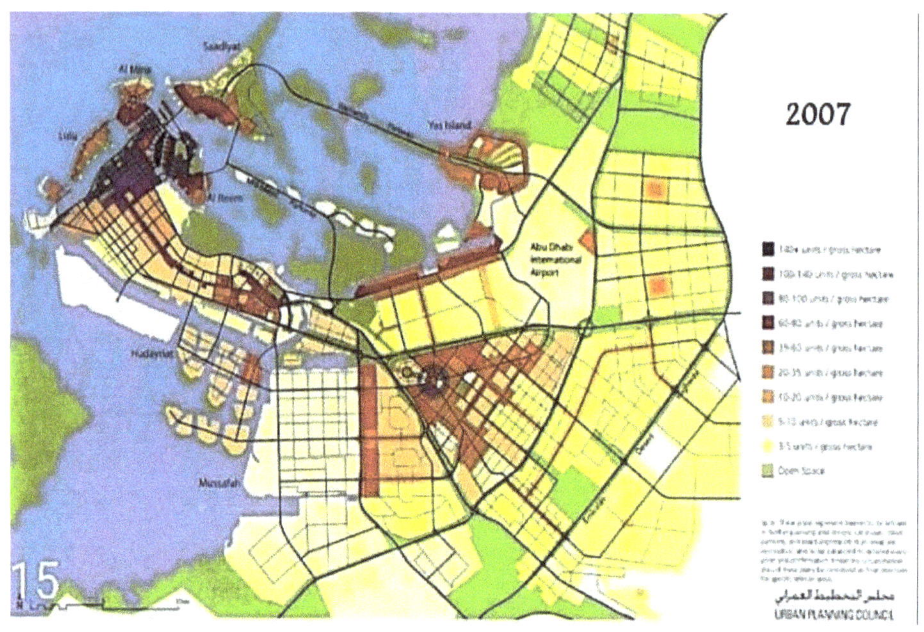

2030 Master Plan (UPC)

(2007- 2030) Program where Abu Dhabi Urban Planning Council (UPC) was established to define the Abu Dhabi Emirate Planning needs and provide sustainable development factors up to 2030.

Today, when I look at the past, I say that Sheikh Zayed (RIP) was long-sighted. He rushed in a race against time and achieved the great ambitions of his people. The first thing in his mind was to focus on the urgent needs of his people and Abu Dhabi City, to be the Political Capital of the United Arab Emirates.

Photo source: Fadel Al Muhairi

Chapter 1: H.H Sheikh Zayed The UAE Founder

Sheikh Zayed's Profile:

His Highness, Sheikh Zayed Bin Sultan Al Nahyan (RIP)

His Highness, Sheikh Zayed Bin Sultan Al Nahyan (RIP), was born in 1918. He was the youngest of his three brothers, Sheikh Shakhboot (RIP), Sheikh Hazza (RIP), and Sheikh Khalid (RIP). Their mother, Sheikha Salama Bint Butti, daughter of the leader of the Al-Qubeisat tribe., Zayed was influenced by his beloved mother in his childhood, who breast-fed him the milk of glory and magnanimity. H.H remained obedient with her, keen to satisfy her until she moved to the top companion in Abu Dhabi in 1970. Learned on her hands God bless, generosity, giving attention to the community, helping the sick and needy, and respecting the elderly. These interests were reinforced in Her Highness, his wife, Sheikha.

Fatima Bint Mubarak, the mother of the Emiratis (Um Al Emarat), has the same qualities of Faith, the right approach, and the unlimited love of the UAE homeland and citizens.

In His Highness father's Majlis, Sheikh Zayed learned the way of ruling and the relationship between the ruler and his people. Learned about Bedouin morals, customs, and urban traditions and situations. The Majlis also taught him the style of Arab hospitality, tolerance, and respect for the elderly. Since his childhood, he has been passionate about reading the biography of the Prophet Muhammad (PBUH), the facts of history and events that have passed through and around the Arabian Peninsula. Zayed was The Worrier Leader! When he became in power, he regained his old memories and insisted to attain the highest level of achievements, supported by his native followers and plenty of friends worldwide.

"No value for wealth unless used to serve and delight the people," said Sheikh Zayed, the Ruler of Abu Dhabi and UAE President (RIP).

Zayed The Beloved Personality:

H.H Sheikh Zayed loved his homeland and developed it inch by inch. Zayed was a man of development and growth.

Sheikh Zayed was not only the Ruler of the Abu Dhabi Emirate or the President of the UAE. He was an Arab National Leader who worked on Arab Nation Unity.

Moreover, He was an international figure that won the World Awards and pride for his country, the UAE, and Arab and Islamic Nation!

Sheikh Zayed, Kamal Hamza, and Brigadier General Dr. Qalander,

He was smiling at everyone's face before he knew who he is!

He asks you before you ask him:

This photograph was published in the Book of Eng. Kamal Hamza recounts his experience with the founder, Sheikh Zayed (RIP), and his photographs collected with him, including this picture, means to Hamza a lot, "It Highlights the extent of affection and emotional warmth that Sheikh Zayed used to bear to others regardless of race or colour. He was engaged with the warmth of the spontaneous love and generosity of Zayed the Father."

The photograph was taken in 1972 during a trip on the Nile River during His Highness' visit to Sudan, accompanied by Brigadier General Dr. Qalander, the governor of Khartoum City" at that time.

Zayed the Green Hands:

Green House Vegetables from Sadiyat Island in 1969.

The Greenhouse Photo source: Ali Bushnaq

That was Abu Dhabi Arid Land Research Center of the Dewan headed by the Late Abdullah Kaddas, Agricultural adviser in Abu Dhabi Royal Diwan, in cooperation with the University of Arizona to produce vegetables such melon, tomatoes, and cucumber.

The project started at Al Sadiyat Island in 1969. Vegetation was grown in plastic water pipes injected with desalinated water and fertiliser without using soil. Its cost was $3 Million. It was called the Green House, visited by Sheikh Zayed in 1970 and later same year together with the Somalian and Gabon Presidents.

Photo source: Ali Bushnaq

The most remarkable visit to the greenhouse cooled by the water evaporation process was by Mohammed Ali In 1974.

Photo source: Ali Bushnaq

International media concentrated on the National Geographic report about producing vegetables in arid lands and the white sand of the desert in Abu Dhabi. The project GM manager was Dr. Reighly, followed by Dr. Merle Jensen, the project manager who headed the project and trained well 26 manpower and lived at Al Sadiyat Island with his family up to 1975. The greenhouse was producing more than 350 tons of vegetables per year, managed by Mr Bushnaq. Later the Greenhouse was shifted, and another greenhouse was built on Madinat Zayed – Liwa Road in 1979.

Zayed (RIP) was the first head of state to receive the Golden Panda Award in 1996.

His Highness as President of UAE obtained the Gold Panda Certificate from the Global Environment Fund in recognition of his unlimited success in the field of environment and all greenery related matters.

This led to a clean and pure environment, from the green land to pure water, combating desertification with afforestation and natural reserves, preserving endangered species of birds and animals, and considering Sir Bani Yas Island as a model for nature reserves to protect wildlife and development.

The hand that changed the White sand of the desert into Colourful Greenery!

Palm Tree, The Tree of Paradise!

His Highness, Sheikh Zayed (RIP), felt very comfortable and happy when he waters the palm trees himself.

The palm is a blessed tree that God created for his people in life and His worshippers in the life after. It is the tree of paradise that our beloved Virgin Mary has shaken.

There are more than 40 million palm trees in the UAE, of which 16.5 million trees are fruitful, producing 750 thousand tons per year, according to the statistics made by the Ministry of Agriculture and Fisheries in 2004.

The number of palm trees and production has certainly risen during the 17 years that passed after that date of statistics.

Photo Source: The Author

This palm tree has a story known only by a few people. It was begotten out of an old mother palm and currently still standing in its mother's grave inside the garden of Sheikh Zayed, the first mosque, opposite the Cultural Foundation in Abu Dhabi.

In 1969, Sheikh Zayed's order was issued to preserve the palm trees, not to be exposed, and not to be uprooted in any way. Even those old palm trees that were planted by the municipality. Eng. Suroory, head of the Agriculture Section, instructed his team to make cement belts around each old palm tree to prevent falling from wind or accidental forms.

The instructions were to keep trees of all kinds and intensify the plantation of roundabouts and the central islands of main streets, to transform Abu Dhabi into a green carpet and a lush garden.

The Palm tree embraces Abu Dhabi Municipality Mosque's Minaret.

Snapshot by the colleague/ Reabal Al-Khateeb

In his book, "Zayed... Omer The Third", the author Dr. Mohammed al-Qudsi says that, "Sheikh Zayed (RIP) planted 280 million trees in the arid desert. H.H was in love with the greenery that was rolled over his beloved country. How humble you were, dear Dad!"

Zayed The UAE Founder:

H.H Sheikh Zayed, H.E Sheikh Hamdan, Discusing The Islamic Science Institute

To develop the Emirate of Abu Dhabi and its suburbs, the Planning Council, chaired by His Highness, and the membership of Sheikh Mohammed Bin Khalifa (RIP), and the later's sons Sheikhs Hamdan, Tahnoon, and Saif, in addition to his brother Sheikh Khalid Bin Sultan (RIP), and the director of finance Mr. Thompson was formed.

All this was to advise the council members regarding the development of the Emirate of Abu Dhabi. In the same decree, H.H invited the consulting engineers and other government officials to attend Planning Council meetings when needed, to take their technical advice, and move the Emirate forward at a steady and thoughtful pace towards progress and prosperity.

Thus, His Highness Sheikh Zayed deserved the title of (Zayed The Founder), and his name was recorded on the purest   pages of history with the golden text.

Zayed and Education:

The education process has seen successive progress in the number of schools and the teaching staff.

In 1948, Abu Dhabi had two schools only, one school to the north of Qasr Al-Hisn, known as Khalaf School (Al Otaiba), the second was at Al Dhahar, East to the central market, known as Bin Karam School. Both taught Quran, Arabic language, and Arithmetic.

In 1966, when Sheikh Zayed became the Ruler of Abu Dhabi Emirate, Abu Dhabi had five schools and 528 students, including Al Falahiya school. Al Falahyia School, was a store house for the British Political Agency, to the North East of the Agency, built in 1957 and given to the public to be used as boy school. Unfortunately, Al Falahiya was demolished in 1968 as the site was replaced by two new buildings (Now Landmark Tower). In 1967, Sheikh Zayed established the Department of Education, headed by the Scottish director Dr. Harold Spencer. Evening literacy classes added, supervised by the Department of Education.

The students at that time were working and helping their parents, so Sheikh Zayed thought that the government would give financial allocations to students of different nationalities to encourage them to go to school.

The Government gave great importance to education in constructing kindergartens, schools, literacy centres, universities, higher technical colleges, and commercial and agricultural institutes.

The opening of the Emirates University in Al Ain in 1977 and the Colleges of higher technology for male and female students in Abu Dhabi in 1988, and then Zayed University in 1998, was a great testament to the achievements made to graduate students of science, arts, and technology.

The number of schools in Abu Dhabi for the academic year 2017/2018 was 355 public and private, and the number of students reached 240000 for the same school year.

Zayed's Dreams Come True:

Hazza Al-Mansoori claimed as the first Emirati and Arab astronaut (SFP) to arrive at the International Space Station since its inception in 1998.

"Today, we are witnessing with pride and happiness the beginning of the UAE's first manned mission into space," said Mohammed bin Rashid Space Center Director General Yusuf Hamad Al-Shaibani. Now, Hazaa Al-Mansouri is not only the UAE's first astronaut (SFP) but has become the UAE's ambassador in space, in every sense of the word."

Source: Raseef

H H Sheikha Fatima Bint Mubarak, President of the General Women's Union and the UAE's Supreme Council for Motherhood and Childhood, said, "This is a historic achievement that history will record in gold," WAM reported.

"This good work is thanks to the Founder of the UAE Renaissance, Sheikh Zayed Bin Sultan Al Nahyan," she said, adding "It is a message to all Arab youth that we can move forward and follow others, an event that strengthens the leadership's confidence in the UAE's youth, who carry the flag of thc UAE, which reinforces the aspirations of the UAE's youth. The UAE is promising for the future."

Chapter 2: Al Nahyan Shoulder To Shoulder (1928- Now)

H.H Sheikh Shakhbout Al Nahyan (RIP)

Sheikh Shakhbout was the Ruler of Abu Dhabi Emirate from 1928-1966. In 1966, Sheikh Shakhbout informed his companion Sheikh Mohammed bin Khalifa of his willingness to step down the Emirate of

Abu Dhabi to his brother Sheikh Zayed bin Sultan Al Nahyan. H.H witnessed Abu Dhabi Town Planning Beginnings.

H.H Sheikh Zayed Bin Sultan Al Nahyan UAE Founder, RIP (1966-2004)

H.H Sheikh Khalifa Bin Zayed Al Nahyan UAE President (2004-Now)

H.H Sheikh Mohammed Bin Zayed, Crown Prince De Facto ADE
Ruler (2014-Now)

H.E Sheikh Mohammed Bin Khalifa (1899-1979) RIP, is the grandson of Sheikh Zayed bin Khalifa bin Shakhbout, Zayed the First (1855 – 1909) RIP, from his elder son Sheikh Khalifa RIP.

A peaceful man always smiling, self-satisfied, and all that he cared about was the Life-after. Simple man, God provided himself comfort, knowledge, and contentment. He gathered Al Nahyan Family shoulder to shoulder. His Palace was In front of Qasr Al Hisn Palace.

Chapter 3: Abu Dhabi Culture

Trust, Honesty, Generosity:

Trust, honesty, integrity, and respect were the distinctive qualities in Abu Dhabi and the UAE in general, regardless of race, colour, and nationality.

"In November 1956, after the attack on the Suez Canal, banks in Bahrain were closed, and BP had salaries for its employees that did not arrive in Abu Dhabi," said Wanda Jablonski.

But Tim Hillyard, the Chief BP's Representative in the Trucial States, told his guest, the journalist Wanda Jablonski, "I went to Sheikh Shakhbout and explained to him the company's commitment to pay the salaries on time, and I asked, "Is it possible, would you lend me a sum of money, please?"

"How much do you need?" asked Sheikh Shakhbout.

Tim answered, "£15000…." She continued, "It was only a few hours until I received the money, and Sheikh Shakhbout has not asked the lender for any receipt!!"

As for the ruler, the people were loyal, generous, doing all the good, and helping the needy. No matter who the person and the nationality he carries, there was no discrimination. Moreover, it was mentioned that the UAE citizen, Omeir Bin Yousef (RIP), rescued British Airways (BOAC) from a financial crisis once and gave them a loan of £40 million without interest. Mr. Khalil Ailaboni mentioned this incident. The Former Secretary of His Excellency, Dr. Mani Saeed Al Otaiba, inhuman qualities justify the allocation of 30% of his book, Abu Dhabi…The Beginning. These were the income to humanitarian assistance, internally and externally, to rescue the UAE's general anxiety affected by crucial natural crises anywhere.

N.B: Wanda Jablonski, correspondent of the American Newspaper Petroleum Week 1957.

Camel the Desert's Ship:

Camel is a symbol of heritage in Abu Dhabi, UAE, and the Arabian Gulf. Studies indicated that the presence of camels in Abu Dhabi dates back to 3000 BC, according to the excavations at Um Al Nar Island in Abu Dhabi and Helli in Al Ain. There is a passionate relation between the camel and his owner.

Abu Dhabi witnessed the single-hump camel, which was known as Arabic Camel, though there were a limited number of the two-hump Persian camels. Camels have gained a distinctive place in Bedouin life throughout history due to the camel's patience under harsh desert weather!

Passionate relation between the camel and his owner

The camel was usually used to carry weights, ride, trade and transportation, the reason it was called "Desert's Ship." They were the main source of meat, dairy, leather and lint, i.e., the Bedouins rely on it to have all their needs of food, drink, house furniture, and hand knitting industries. This is why camels were the indicator of the economic situation and prestige. Even women's dories were paid from the past's good and rare types of white and black camels.

His Highness Sheikh Zayed paid special attention to the breeding of camels and encouraged UAE citizens through camel races. The number of camels increased in Abu Dhabi from 44,000 in 1983 to 187 thousand camels in 2003.

Camels transporting firewood

In these photos taken in the 1960s, we observe how the camel was transporting firewood from Al Buraimi and Liwa Oasis to the neighboring areas with the intention of trading and earning, to meet the needs of the family, or moving their dwelling luggage from one place to another.

UAE Heritage:

Zayed Heritage Village was founded by the blessed father, Sheikh Zayed bin Sultan Al-Nahyan (RIP). Constructed in 1989, officially opened in 2001, and honored on 29/10/1994. One of the objectives set at the time of establishment was to educate the new generations about the life of their parents and grandparents, linking them to their customs and traditions and introducing them to their heritage and history through the exhibits, possessions, acquisitions, a book published, and events held on the ground. All sections that embody the life, in the past, on mainland, marine, and farms. Since then, best efforts have been done to provide significant services to the nation.

Heritage Revival Committee had many sincere men and members during the past few years, such as Thani bin Mohammed Bin Thani Al Rumaithi, Ali Bin

Salem Al Kaabi, Mohammed Bin Saeed Al-Haely, Ateeq Al Falasi, Dalmook Al Mehairi, and many personnel, who contributed their efforts to establish this Heritage Village with its sections that represent all aspects of life in Abu Dhabi old days. Mr. Thani Bin Mohammed Bin Thani Al-Rumaithi, a member of the Heritage Village, has a lot of knowledge and excellent meanings of words used by the seamen, bedouins in the mainland, and urban inhabitants of Abu Dhabi shores in the past. Even the detailed meaning of names and tools used in the past daily life. One of the most active women fond of UAE heritage I do appreciate Miss Fatima Al Mansoori, Director of Zayed Center for Studies and Research, Emirates. Heritage Club.

The Burjeel:

The Burjeel structure wooden and cloth

The people of the Gulf were the first to invent natural cooling and air conditioning in the burning desert.

The Burjeel structure, whether it was wooden/ cloth or concrete, is an air collector allowing the wind to circulate inside the room. This is exactly like the open round tin used to ignite the fire for the barbecue. Burjeel is a natural ventilation structure that looks like the cap at the tops of the houses. It was adopted by British petroleum engineers when they constructed their old rest houses in the Abu Dhabi harbour in the past, which became part of the British Club (The Club) later. It was also adopted in Abu Dhabi Old Airport in the 1960s and in the old houses in Das Island. It tells us that "The need is the mother of invention."

The Burjeel structure concrete and cloth

The Ruler's Hand Stick:

The Ruler's Hand Stick

Cities like individuals have a specific date of birth. H.H Sheikh Zayed managed the UAE political transformation and the construction of Abu Dhabi town to be the capital city, using his long experience in Al-Ain as the Ruler's representative (1946-1966).

Frankly speaking, Sheikh Zayed was the real Town Planner, the Supervisor, the Landlord, and the Gardener.

The Ruler's Hand Stick

He used to carry his stick as a drawing instrument. He marked his vision and planned on the sand. With his stick, Sheikh Zayed has drawn the finest lines and pointed to the perfect project locations.

Lines turned into roads, roundabouts and maps turned into schools, hospitals, police stations, mosques, etc.

He was meeting Abu Dhabi's chief town planner, Mr. Takahashi (RIP), carrying a hand stick and asking, "What is this? How many government departments will be there? What are the site dimensions, and the reason for planning the Administration Complex next to Al Hisn Palace, the official residence of the Ruler?"

H. H asked by his hand stick about the future use, the land use, and the types of lands that can be granted to his people to ensure a happy life for them and their coming children.

Zayed's hand stick was blessed because the hand which carried it was a green hand. He planned Abu Dhabi's present situation and its bright prosperous future to be the rest house and park where the inhabitants feel happy and joyful.

Diving (Al Ghous):

Though diving was the profession of the Gulf people in the past, it was subjected to some crisis and depression in the late 1920s, where Japanese artificial pearls and the global economic crisis emerged since 1929.

Pearl Diving Team Onboard

The late Hamad Al Qamzi described the 1940s in an interview with Al Itihad Newspaper in 1984:

"With the exception of tribal chiefs, major merchants, and some of the arrivals from Persia, all Bani Yas with its branches of tribes in Abu Dhabi, as well as 70% of the residents of Al Ain were only working in diving and the trade of pearls and fishing. Even the excluded groups, although stay in the cities, had their main source of income from diving and the sea. When he was six or seven years old, the child was not found in the country, as his father accompanied him for training, and get qualification for work. From early morning until sunset, divers were collecting oysters and then, on the evening, the quantities were sent to the back of the ship. The Galalees (children) were awaken early in the morning to extract the pearls from the shells. The recession intensified during the Second World War. The workers were going out into the sea but the payoff was poor. The area was cut off from food and clothing, and the presence of money meant nothing. The markets were free of dates, rice and other things. People became in famine where the population was dependent on the outside and they had nothing to eat."

Pearl diving fleets continued to sail each year in search of natural pearls, but the already scarce return of divers was descending. It became clear that this ancient profession had begun to die silently and come to its inevitable end in the 1940s.

Al Yasat Community (Al Fareej):

Historically, the largest gathering of tribes was in Al Dhahr area.

Al Dhahar was at the mid-island, on the north shore where "Al Fardha" was the port, and the old market with its narrow passage was covered with tents.

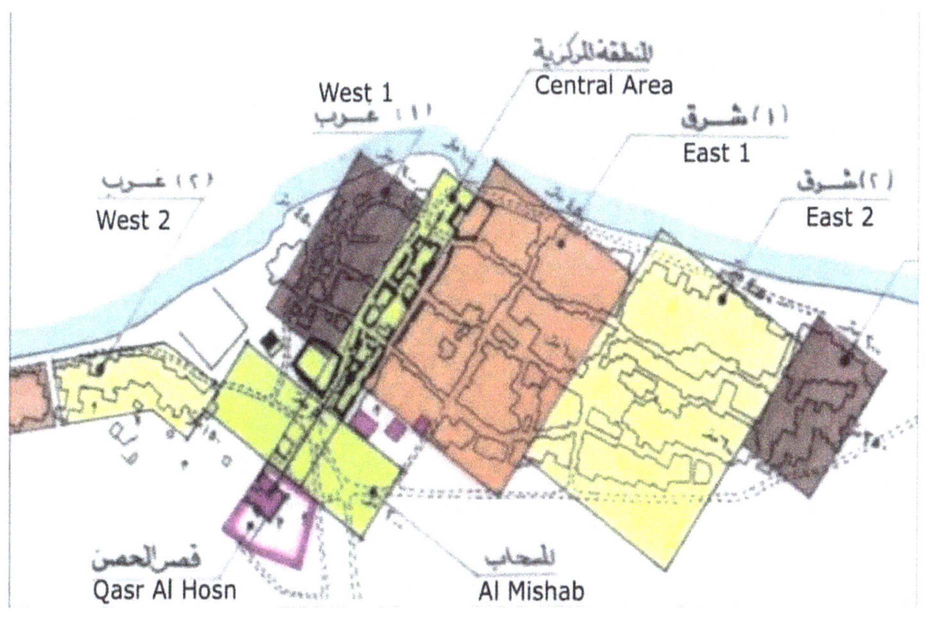

Bani Yas tribes distribution map East and West (Dr. Makhlouf)

The Bani Yas tribes were distributed at Al Dhahr area, and each tribe or (Fareej) had proximity with the people of neighbouring Fareej despite the difficulty of moving in the hot weather.

Sheikh Shakhbout bin Sultan's policy was that every citizen had to live with his tribe. It was H.H policy to house people with his family or tribe in their designated area. For this reason, he asked any of the tribes living in Al Ain to have a house in Al Ain to remain with his group, not weakened or covered by another power in case of any offense.

Abu Dhabi's old town consisted of unique Fareej or residential neighbourhoods, including:

- Al-Sheikhs' Fareej: Qasr Al Hosn, which is the palace of the ruler and his family, and around it are houses belonging to some members of the royal family and their relatives where located around the Mosque of Al Otaibat, the oldest mosque in Abu Dhabi built by the merchant Khalaf Bin Otaiba and his son Ahmed bin Khalaf.

- Al-Rumaithat Fareej: It was located near Al Hadd, known as Al Ramaithat Hadd, to the west of Al-Arian houses and east of the palm tree belonging to someone of Al Rumaithat, including Sultan bin Rashid.

- Al-Qubaisat Fareej: East of the old market and west of Al Rumaithat.

- Al-Hawamel's Fareej: It was inhabited by families of Hawamel El Yasat tribe and located between the old market and Qasr Al Hosn.

- Al-Maharba's Fareej: Families belonging to the Al Mahareba Al Yasat tribe, located west of the old market and Qasr Al Hosn.

- Al-Qamzan's Fareej: Inhabited by families belonging to Al Qamzan El Yasat tribe, located west of the market, to Qasr Al Hosn near Fareej Al Maharba, Al-Hawamel, and Al-Qubaisat.

- Al-Mazari's Fareej: This neighborhood was located west and north of the fort of Qasr Al Hosn.

- Al-Otaibat Fareej: The families belonging to the Otaibat El Yasat tribe lived in Hadd Al-Otaibat area, which is attributed to them for the presence of their own bander and their own diving ships.

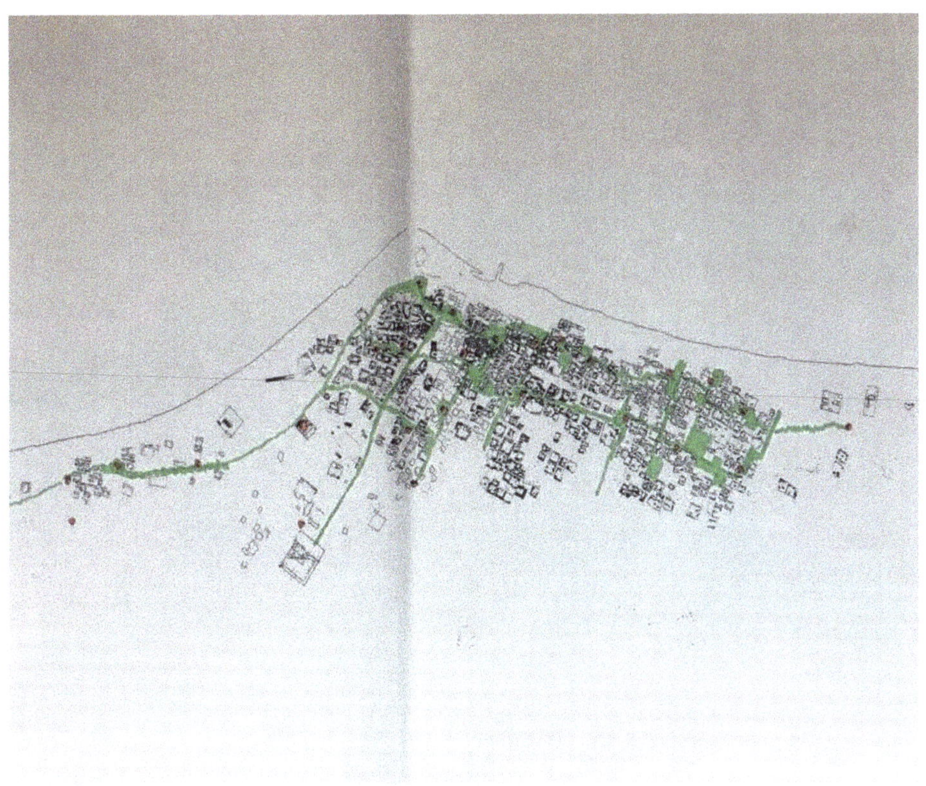

Darb Al Khair Pedistrian (Mosques Distribution) From East to West

The sites of the mosques chosen in such a long way from east to west we can call it (Darb Al Khair), crossing the tribes' Fareejs (Al Furjan).

As for Al-Bateen, it was located as mentioned on the western side of Abu Dhabi Island. The old village of Al-Bateen had had been replaced by public houses handed over in 1967-68 and later demolished when the area was replanned in the 1980s to become two-storey residential villas.

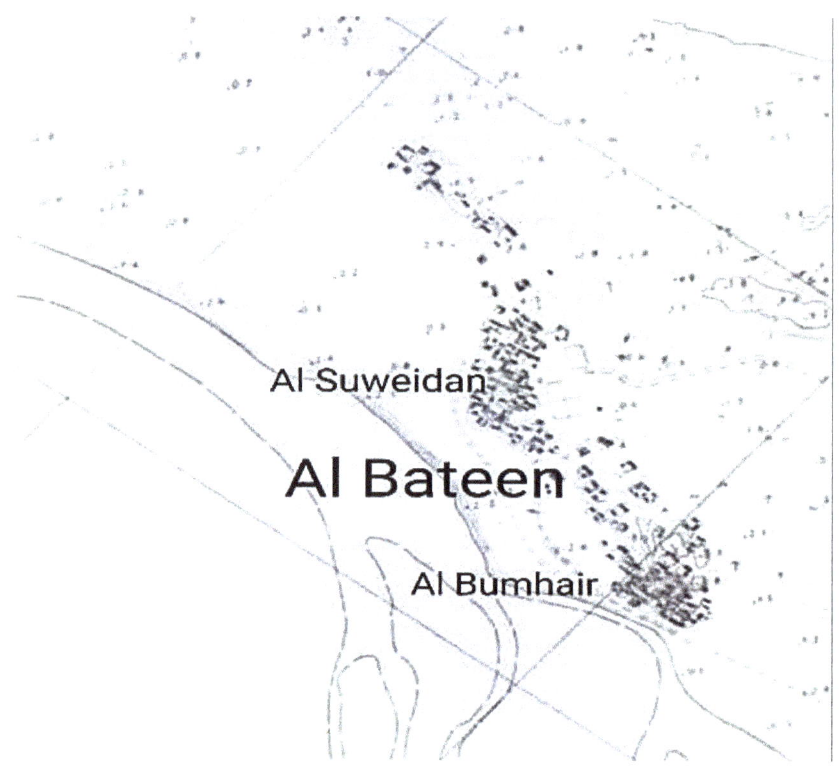

Al Bateen Tribe Distribution map (Al Suweidan and Al Bumhair)

The earlier residents of Al-Bateen are from Al-Suweidan and Al Bou mhair, who worked in fishing, shipbuilding, and diving. Their old boats are still scattered on the nearby shore of Khor al-Bateen, telling the story of the past. Well known men of Al Suwaidan al Mutawa and the venerable man Sheikh Khalifa bin Ahmed Al-Suweidi, the poet Majid bin Saeed al-Suweidi, the greatest of his time and the poet Mohammed bin Hamid al-

Suweidi, who worked as a guard at Qasr Al Hisn and then a guard of Al Maqta fort during the rule of Sheikh Shakhbut (RIP).

- Al-Suweidan's Fareej: Most of the families belonging to the Suweidi tribe El Yasat lived in the area of Al-Bateen.

- Al Buomhir Fareej: It was located near Fareej Al-Suweidan in the Al-Bateen area, home to Al Bumhair El Yasat Tribe families.

Al-Bateen is now a high-end neighborhood. It is surrounded by greenery because of its proximity to the Al Khubeira district, the Intercontinental Hotel, the Crown Prince's Diwan and the Central Bank.

Info Narration Source: (Thani Bin Mohammed Bin Thani Al Rumaithi)

Chapter 4: Abu Dhabi Old Days

Sas Al Nakhl Archaeology:

1959: Um Al Nar (Sas Al Nakhl) archaeological discovery.

Sixty-two years have passed since antiquities were first discovered on Um Al-Nar Island in 1959 by a Danish Archaeological Team. The Um Al-Nar site was the first archaeological site to be excavated in Abu Dhabi. Sheikh Shakhbout, accompanied by his cousin Sheikh Mohammed Bin Khalifa, opened the area for excavation in 1959.

Um Al Nar (Sas Al Nakhl) Ruins 1959

Studies have shown that this civilisation has extended for about (2700-2000 BC) and was flourishing with the evidence of residential settlements and extensive commercial and cultural relations with the Al Rafidain Valley populations interested in copper, pottery, and stoneware. H.H Sheikh Zayed welcomed the Danish team and strongly supported their findings documented.

The Trucial States before Oil:

A quick look at events before oil in Emirates, we mark the following:

1820: The British campaign on al-Qawasim.

1823: The treaty became known as the (Trucial Coast), under which Indian and British armies withdrew from local affairs and limited their mission to defend and guarantee the freedom of navigation.

1930: RAF airstrip was established. During World War II, RAF and USAF aircraft landed in the Gulf region.

1932: Oil appeared in Bahrain, features of change began in most areas of the Gulf, and British-run courts to judge on cases involving non-Arab foreigners. The aim was to protect the British themselves and the allied Indian nationals. Some permanent staff worked in the courts, and British judges regularly visited to decide cases. With the arrival of several foreign companies, the situation has changed. The British found themselves faced with two options:

a) Either they should deploy more staff and judges

or hand over the courts to the local authorities. They chose to extend their influence by increasing the number of staff and judges. That is to establish permanent courts visited periodically by judges. Bahrain was the political and military command centre of the Gulf region.

World War II passed through the Gulf sheikhdoms peacefully. An airstrip has been set up in Dubai. Another airstrip in Sharjah to accommodate aircraft from India and the Far East. By 1948, the people of the Trucial coast had forgotten World War II. One of its features was the distribution of aid such as sugar, rice, and basic foodstuffs, although the war deepened the economic hardship that began in 1929.

1948: Great Britain limited its air presence to two bases, Bahrain and Sharjah, each operating a range of ground services led by an officer. Since then, warplanes have no longer existed permanently in the Gulf region.

Before India's independence in 1947, the Arab side of the Gulf, except for Saudi Arabia and Iraq, was under the British administration in India. It was governed in a somewhat similar way by the system of the independent Emirate, which is usually ruled by maharaja and, along with British Agents, to provide advice. The situation in the Gulf was a little bit different, perhaps because the British Government in India was concerned about interfering in the local affairs of the Gulf sheikhdoms.

The British Government has not interfered in the local affairs of the Trucial coast and has provided it with the protection of the security, defence, and maritime safety. In limited periods between 1820 and 1948, the UK felt the need to establish a naval force somewhere in the Gulf because the Bombay Navy carried out security (later The Indian Navy), backed by the Royal Navy.

In the 19th century, there was to be a fleet of six small ships roaming the Gulf sheikhdoms, but that remained a dead letter, as confirmed by the mid-19th-century Memorandum of the British Charter, which complained that no ship had been visited in two years.

The anti-British treaties and the Gulf sheikhdoms have given her Majesty's government considerable influence in exchange for very limited responsibility. This remained the case until the British withdrawal in 1971 and the declaration of the establishment of the United Arab Emirates.

Al Maqta Crossing Way:

Al Maqta Crossing Way 1953

Khan Sahib Company carried out this temporary crossing of Al Maqta in favour of Petroleum Development (Trucial Coast) Ltd. for 1,000 pounds in 1952. It was opened by H.E Sheikh Hamdan Bin Mohamed Al

Nahyan and used until 1968 when Al Maqta metallic bridge was completed. Khan Sahib Company was hired to be the supplier of oil fields and implement the construction contracts for Abu Dhabi oil company PD (TC) Ltd. It was the only company owning heavy equipment. Latter followed by Santa Fe, Gray McKenzie, and Caterpillar. It offers the lowest prices and the finest finishing.

Mr. Hussein Imad Al Mtairi (Khan Sahib), origin from the Saudi Mtair tribe, settled on the Emirati Coast. He was appointed as the National agent of the British Government with (Khansahib) as Title. He didn't continue in his political position for long. Hussain Imad (Khansahib) owned a national contracting company that executed many major projects, including Al Maqta Crossing in Abu Dhabi opened in 1953." (*Info source: Hussein Albadi*)

Al Maqta Metalwork Bridge:

*Al Maqta Metalwork Bridge **1966***

His Highness the Ruler Sheikh Shakhbout bin Sultan Al-Nahyan
(RIP) and Consult Canadian with the help of PD (TC) Ltd oil company.

بسم الله الرحمن الرحيم

الاتفاقية

*Agreement for the construction of Al Maqta bridge in Arabic dated
2/12/1965*

It looks that December 2nd is always the luckiest day because, in 1971, it marks the National Independence Day of the United Arab Emirates!

The photograph above, taken from Wagner Biro's Site for Al Maqta Bridge, was erected and completed by them in 1967 and officially opened on 6/8/1968. Santa Fe transported the steelwork and supplied their cranes for the Bridge builder "Wagner Biro".

The main contractor, the Canadian Cansult, won the competition, which was held by the British Consultant Bryan Colquhoun, between the following invited contractors:

1- Gammon Gulf is owned by the Bahraini Yousef Al Obeidli.

2- Contracting and Trading (CAT) owned by the Lebanese Emil Al Busstani.

3- AST Abroad Dubai.

4- Cansult Ltd, the Canadian Enterprise represented by Eng. Raymond.

The Canadian Cansult was headed by Bob Wintzel. It was the first contracting project of Cansult in Abu Dhabi in 1965.

Al Maqta Bridge is approximately 300 metres long, the maximum span distance of the bridge is 90m. The upper structure consists of steel sheets to provide 4- lane road, two lanes 10 ft wide for each direction. (Extra steel stretching arc), with a thread, the surface was made. The total steel weight of the bridge was almost 1400 tons.

Wagner Biro is an Austrian company that received authorization to trade in iron in 1854 by Rudolph Philipp Wagner. Wagner-Biro was founded when the locksmith Anton Biró and Albert Milde & Co. amalgamated.

"The order of Al Maqta bridge in Abu Dhabi in 1964 marks the start of Wagner-Biro's entry into the Arab market. Since then, Wagner-Biro has been operating from a subsidiary in Abu Dhabi and shortly after that in Dubai. The 1967 Al Maqta bridge established the first connection between Abu Dhabi Island and the mainland."

Abu Dhabi Year to Year Calender:

- 1761: The year of the discovery of fresh water in Abu Dhabi Island.

- 1790: The year Abu Dhabi was declared the capital of Bani Yas instead of the Al Mariyah /Liwa.

- 1818: The year Sheikh Shakhbout Bin Dhiab Al-Nahyan was nominated as Ruler of the Emirate of Abu Dhabi, succeeded his son, Tahnoun Bin Shakhbout Al-Nahyan.

- 1855: The year of the announcement of Sheikh Zayed Bin Khalifa (Zayed Al-Kabeer) as ruler of the Emirate of Abu Dhabi.

- 1901: The photographer Samuel Zwimer arrived in Abu Dhabi and took photos to Al Hisn Fort.

- 1928: The year of Sheikh Shakhbout Bin Sultan al-Nahyan's appointment as ruler of the Emirate of Abu Dhabi.

- 1935: The year of the establishment of an RAF airstrip in Sir Bani Yas.

- 1939: The year of establishing The Oil Development Company (Trucial Coast) Ltd. (ADPC) later.

- 1948: The year of Abu Dhabi-Dubai border talks.

- 1950: The first drilling for oil well at Ras Al Sadr without success.

- 1952: The US Company Superior has waived oil exploration rights in Abu Dhabi offshore. Abu Dhabi tasked British and French companies, and BP and Total have agreed to establish ADMA- Opco.

- 1952: The year Abu Dhabi has a population of 4,000.

- 1955: The year of the construction of the first airstrip on Abu Dhabi Island.

- 1962: Hana Khraish, a Lebanese contractor, gets the first hotel building permit belonging to Khalifa Bin Hammad rented to the Othman Bank.

- 1956: Honer Cowell (Mrs. Cuthbert) arrived in Abu Dhabi and lived with her husband Ian Cuthbert, BP representative, on Abu Dhabi Corniche. She left in 1960.

- 1957: Miss Wanda Jablonski, the Petroleum Weekend journalist, arrived in Abu Dhabi to cover the oil discovery news.

- 1958: The year of oil discovery in the Emirate of Abu Dhabi.

- 1959: The British Bank of the Middle East (BME), now HSBC, opened its branch in Abu Dhabi.

- 1961: Beach hotel was built in Abu Dhabi managed by CAT Company.

- 1962: Halcrow/ Scott Wilson Kerk Patrick Abu Dhabi designed Abu Dhabi directive plan.

- 1962: The year of the export of the first commercial shipment of oil from Das Island.

- 1962: Tamer Salameh arrived from CAT company in Bahrain and started car, A/C, refrigerators, trading.

- 1962: Main contractors in Abu Dhabi Town Atto (Victor Hashim), Al Darwish, CAT (Emil Al Busstani), Al Masoud and Sons, Rashed Owaidha, Mohammed Al Hur, Ahmed Al Suweidi, Hmooda Bin Ali, Thani Bin Murshed, Khamis Al Muhairi, Ghanim Al Qubaisi, Hassan Nassriyah, and many more.

- 1963: Sheikh Shakhbout appointed the accountant of the Othman Bank Ali Buti as postmaster instead of the British Bank.

- 1964: The Abu Dhabi BBME Branch banker, Mr. Riley, left Abu Dhabi to join Midland Bank in the UK.

- 1965: The British Agent in Abu Dhabi Colonel Hugh Boustead retired, and Sheikh Zayed appointed him as horse stables Master in Mazyed, where he stayed till his death in 1980 (RIP).

- 1966: Sheikh Zayed Bin Sultan Al-Nahyan, the ruler of Abu Dhabi Emirate.

- 1967: Sheikh Zayed issued the decree to establish the Department of Civil Aviation in Abu Dhabi.

- 1967: William Robertson appointed as manager of Abu Dhabi Harbour.

- 1968: The Year of the Abu Dhabi and Dubai Federation with Emirate population 46,375 and AD city population 22,000.

- 1970: Al Bateen Airport was officially opened by Sheikh Zayed Bin Sultan as ruler of Abu Dhabi Emirate.

- 1971: Etisalat Building (Abu Dhabi Telephone and Telegraph Co.) opened at Airport Road Sector W4.

- 1972: Sheikh Zayed visited Um Al Nar (Sas Al Nakh) Island and ordered the construction of an Oil Refinery.

- 1972: Sheikh Zayed ordered to build the Corniche Maternity Hospital.

- 1974: Agreement to build the Beach Hospital in Abu Dhabi.

- 1974: Sheikh Zayed ordered to build Abu Dhabi Sports City opposites Al Bateen Airport.

- 1974: First Broadcasting of Abu Dhabi coloured TV.

- 1975: Agreement to build Abu Dhabi Intercontinental Hotel.

- 1975: Agreement to make Abu Dhabi Gulf Hotel ($ 23 million).

- 1976: Omer Al Khayam (Now Al Hamra Hotel) on Electra Street caught fire.

- 1979: Agreement to construct Al Mafraq Hospital (AED 232 million). Also, Al Mafaq Sewage Purification plant (AED 246 million).

- 1977: Traffic Signals, and Over Fly pedestrian passage across Khalifa Street.

- 1978: Al Musaffah Bridge constructed.

- 1978: Abu Dhabi-Dubai highway constructed.

- 1978: Sheikh Zayed ordered to construct Al Mushref Women and Kids Park (Now Um Al Emarat Park)

- 1981: The year of the first meeting of the Gulf Cooperation Council (GCC) in Abu Dhabi, the UAE is considered the founding member of the Cooperation Council.

- 1982: Abu Dhabi International Airport opened 40 kms outside Abu Dhabi Island.

- 1988: Higher Colleges of Technology established in Abu Dhabi.

- 1989: The Abu Dhabi Main Bus Terminal designed by Bulgar Consult and built by Zakum Contracting Co. opened.

- 1990: The year Sheikh Rashed Bin Saeed Al-Maktoum, Ruler of Dubai, died. His name was given Abu Dhabi's Airport Street to become (Rashed Bin Saeed Street).

- 1991: The year of the collapse of BCCI International Bank's portfolio in Abu Dhabi.

- 1994: Baynouna Tower erected in Abu Dhabi.

- 1998: Al Maqta bridge doubled into twins.

- 2001: Abu Dhabi Mall and Marina Mall under Construction.

- 2003: Al Etihad Airways as a National Airlines established.

- 2005: Qasr Al Emarat Hotel started operation.

- 2007: Abu Dhabi National Exhibition Center (ADNEC) opened.

- 2009: Khalifa Bridge between Abu Dhabi and Saadiyat Islands constructed.

- 2010: Sheikh Zayed Bridge, designed by Architect Zaha Hadid was built. Ferrari at Yas Island and SkyTower at Al Reem Island built.

- 2011: Capital Gate Hotel adjacent to ADNEC opened, and Al Etihad Towers at Al Bateen were constructed.

- 2012: Landmark Tower at Abu Dhabi Corniche and Al Huderiyat Bridge was constructed 480 meters long.

- 2014: Yas Mall at Yas Island opened for customers. The University of New York at Al Saadiyat Island opened.

- 2014: Opening of Yas Mall

- 2015: Solar plane launched from Abu Dhabi Airport around the globe

- 2016: Reading Year in the UAE

- 2017: Louvre museum opened in Abu Dhabi

- 2018: Opening of the Al Hosn Palace to the public and the politicians.

- 2019: Hazaa Al-Mansouri first Emirates to climb spacecraft.

- 2020: Opening of the canal (Al Qana) tourist aquarium, restaurants, shopping center, cinema, and bodybuilding at a distance of 2.400 Kms.

Chapter 5: Abu Dhabi Oil Exploration

ADPC (Abu Dhabi Petroleum Company):

ADNOC Onshore Complex, Abu Dhabi Corniche 2020

Since late 1950s, Abu Dhabi's Black Gold River still running!

In January 1936, William Williamson of the Iraqi Petroleum Company (IPC) signed a temporary oil exploration agreement for two years in Abu Dhabi. Thus, the Iraqi Petroleum Company established a subsidiary company named Petroleum Development (Trucial Coast) Ltd. In Jan 1939, Petroleum Development (Trucial Coast) Ltd. signed a long term concessions agreement, followed by exploratory drilling at Ras Al Sader in 1950. In 1957 the same company drilled in Sharjah, at Al Juaiza area, but no oil was discovered.

PD (TC) Ltd Health Center at Juaiza, Sharjah 1957:

In 1959, oil was found at Mirban Well# 3 in Al Dhafra (Western Religion) of Abu Dhabi Emirate. In the early 1960s, Petroleum

Development (Trucial Coast) Ltd. announced the first commercial oil discovery at Bab Oil Field. In 1962, the Company was renamed as Abu Dhabi Petroleum Company (ADPC). The first tanker carrying oil from ADPC Fields was launched from Jebel Al Dhanna terminal in 1963.

In 1965, ADPC signed a 50/50 revenue sharing agreement with Abu Dhabi Government. On the other hand, Sheikh Zayed established the Abu Dhabi National Oil Company (ADNOC) in 1971. In January 1973, the Government of Abu Dhabi acquired a 25% interest. And on December 1974, ADNOC took 60% off (ADPC) ADCO's share.

In 1978 ADCO was an incorporated company, and since February 1979, ADCO has been responsible for operations in the defined onshore concession area. In 1988, the Supreme Petroleum Council (SPC) was established. The law stated that this new body is the Supreme Authority responsible for the oil industry in Abu Dhabi. Since October 2017, ADNOC has brought together its people, resources, products and services under a unified brand.

Abu Dhabi Company for Onshore Petroleum Operations Ltd. (ADCO) is now working as ADNOC Onshore. Its offices are located on Abu Dhabi Corniche, the same ADCO's historical location.

ADPC's Survey Teams:

The earlier survey teams of Abu Dhabi Petroleum Company ADPC (ADCO Later) were camping at Al Hamra, Al Dhafra region (Western Region formerly) in 1959. As shown from this photograph, the helicopter was apparently used for movement, as it was very difficult to use other means of traffic and transportation because of the moving sand dunes.

ADPC's Survey Team camping in the desert 1964:

At Liwa Oasis, tens of villages (Mahader) are scattered at the foothills of the dunes. The 51 villages are inhabited by Bedouins living with their cattle supported by plenty of water, pasture, and palm trees that yield dates. The Oasis Bedouin's farms were considered as resting and hospitality stations for the survey Teams of ADPC (ADCO) in 1961, working near Asab, Bab, and Habshan Oil wells.

Oil and Gas in Abu Dhabi:

ADCO (now ADNOC onshore), a former ADNOC company, celebrated in 2013 the 50 years golden Jubilee of its first shipment of crude oil from the onshore fields through Jebel Al Dhana.

ADNOC has strengthened its relationships with Canadian companies to achieve their objectives by applying global standards in developing oil, gas and human resources through vocational training centres. ADNOC established one of the world's most important gas complexes after completing the project to increase the capacity of the Habshan complex to 4,500 million cubic feet of gas per day in 2007. The plant was known as the Land Gas Development Project - Phase III south of Habshan.

Since November 2004, Gasco, a company of ADNOC (Now ADNOC), in collaboration with Bechtel in London, has designed a plant in Ruwais to produce ethane gas and polyethene production at the Petrochemical Plant in Ruwais. The plant processed 1,300 million cubic feet per day of F-field gas and produced condensate, in addition to the natural gas liquid, including ethylene.

ADCO (currently ADNOC onshore) has also begun to develop the first phase of Al Dabiya, Rumithia and Shanil fields, which in 2006 reached 110,000 barrels per day. Oil and a network of pipelines began production in the first quarter of 2006 from the arid areas of Abu Dhabi. A refinery announced the signing of a contract with the Abu Dhabi Water and Electricity Authority to supply it with a capacity of 300 MW. After completing refining in June 2001 electrical connection with Abu Dhabi Transport and Control, Company Transco was done.

At that time, the petroleum construction company revealed that it is implementing a project to develop marine light gas for Adama, which is working in cooperation with ABBLG to increase the production of marine light gas in the Fields of Abu Al-Bakhoush and Um al-Chef. On 8th October 2005, Abu Dhabi Gas Industries Co., Ltd. (ADNOC) announced the construction of work for the first phase of expanding the Habshan complex on the British Company Fluor. The project aimed to double the capacity of the associated gas propulsion units resulting from Bab reservoirs and increase sulphur processing capacity to protect the environment, establish additional units, and modernise control systems.

In November 2020, the UAE's Supreme Petroleum Council announced new discoveries of non-conventional oil resources recoverable inland areas estimated at 22 billion barrels of oil, in addition to increasing conventional oil reserves by 2 billion barrels of oil in Abu Dhabi.

<u>ADMA - Opco:</u>

ADMA's first Rig um Al Sheif

After the Emirate of Abu Dhabi won an arbitration suit held in France against the Iraq Petroleum Company (IPC) over the concession for exploration in the maritime areas in 1951, and after Superior Co. waived its exploration rights, BP and the French Petroleum Company (later Total), Abu Dhabi Offshore Company Limited (ADMA), acquired the concession for oil and gas exploration in Abu Dhabi marine.

Oil Rig on Um Al Chef 1958:

ADMA-opco first brought in the famous French marine scientist Jacques Cousteau on his research ship Calpso in a sea reconnaissance operation where the historic diving for pearls took place. In 1958, ADMA began drilling in Um Al-Chef field using an offshore drilling platform.

The Steel drilling rig was made in Germany and finished on August 23rd, 1957. It was the first of its kind in the world. Its journey to Das Island, passing through the Suez Canal, lasted 90 days. The platform was installed in Um al-Chef field by 32 technicians who arrived from Kuwait. Fixing in place was completed on January 12th, 1958. The first oil well in Abu Dhabi's seawater began to be drilled where Mr Cousteau surveyed the seabed. Oil was reached at a depth of about 8,755 feet, and on September 1958, Abu Dhabi Marine Co., Ltd. (ADMA) announced its discovery of oil. However, commercial production at the giant field, about 300 square kilometers, did not begin until 1962, when the Dublin oil tanker loaded its first commercial cargo!

(Info Source: Al Emirates Today)

ADMA's Office Building, Khalifa Street, Abu Dhabi 1960s

ADMA offices were on the ground floor of this nice building built in 1957; behind it was the building of Sheikh Khalid Bin Sultan RIP, designed by the Egyptian architect Dr Kurayem, at Sheikh Khalifa Street.

ADMA_OPCO Building in the 1980s and 1990s was on the east shore of Abu Dhabi Island, south of the Le Méridien Hotel, in the Tourist Club area. The building was demolished by its owner Sheikh Suroor Bin Mohammed Al Nahyan, and changed to the giant Abu Dhabi Mall.

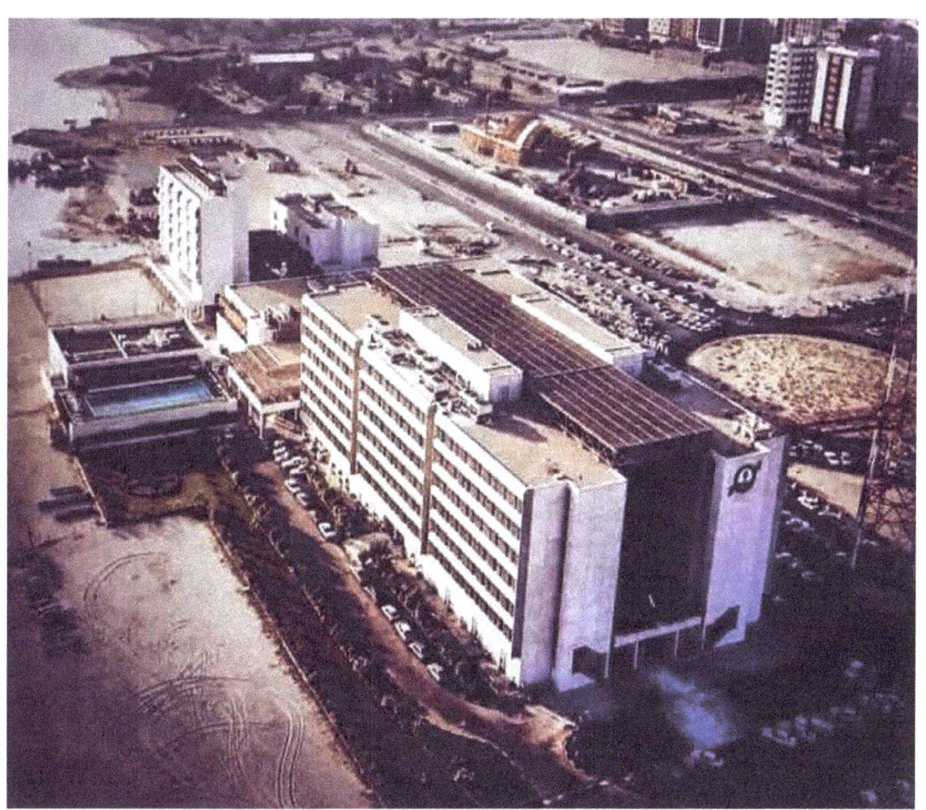

ADMA's Office Building (Sheikh Suroor's property) 80s-90s:

Old ADMA's building had a club and a swimming pool where children used to meet on the weekends. Also, a restaurant where an Indian waiter Babu used to add joy to the customers as he served food at the club.

78

Chapter 6: Abu Dhabi Top 5 Departments

Department of Abu Dhabi Municipality:

Abu Dhabi Municipality was founded in 1961-1962 under the chairmanship of Sheikh Sultan Bin Shakhbout (RIP) and the management of Mr Ismail Badawnah, a Jordanian national (now UAE citizen). It was located on the Corniche next to the Department of Customs, and late in 1967 moved to Al Khalidiya next to Abu Dhabi Department of Finance.

Abu Dhabi Municipality, Abu Dhabi Corniche 1965

The first municipal director under Sheikh Zayed's (RIP) rule was Al-Sunny Banaga, a Sudanese national (1966-1969), followed by Mr Ahmed Awad Al-Karim, also a Sudanese national, who served as assistant director of Abu Dhabi Municipality (1969-1975) and was promoted to the post of Director-General of the Municipality (1975-2004). Mr Al Karim played an active role in developing infrastructure in Abu Dhabi City, which since 1966 was progressing with utmost speed of development and construction.

Abu Dhabi Municipality Staff 1968

The municipality was at the beginning, consisting of basic services sections, including garbage Collection, Commercial Licensing, Land

Registration, and Town Planning. Planning was run by a UK consulting firm (Arabicon) and supervised by a Japanese expert Mr. Takahashi. (1967-1968). The planning task was assigned to Dr Abdulrahman Makhlouf as Director-General of Town Planning in Abu Dhabi Emirate (1968-1976). Then the municipal engineering section, road engineering, agriculture, and sanitation sections were established. Later, set up a food laboratory.

The First Municipal Chairman appointed by H.H Sheikh Zayed (RIP) was H.E Sheikh Saif Bin Mohammed Al Nahyan, followed by His Excellency Sheikh Tahnoun bin Mohammed Al Nahyan, then His Excellency Buti Al-Otaiba, then His Excellency Khalaf Bin Ahmed Al-Otaiba, then His Excellency Sheikh Mohammed Bin Butti Al-Hamed (1974-2006).

My Arrival in Abu Dhabi:

On 13/2/1968, I joined Town Planning Section in Mr Takahachi's office to participate in the drawing preparation of the revised Abu Dhabi Master Plan, based on the grid plan provided by Arabicon, which in turn relied on the basic proposal of the allied consultants, Messrs. Halcrow and Associates/Scott Wilson-Kirk Patrick and Partners In 1962.

In 1968 Abu Dhabi was a small town consisting of a few rows of stone buildings on the beach. Partially demolished city centre, and new buildings scattered on Hamdan and khalifa streets. Other wooden houses were temporarily made of palm fronds.

The stone buildings in Abu Dhabi were very few. The most important was Qasr Al Hosn, the old municipality building built by the Lebanese contractor Hanna Khraish, from the southern Lebanese Ain Ebil village, the customs house building, which was built of mud and coral stones, the British Agency, Al-Otaibat mosque. To the northeast were the Eastern Bank building, the British Bank of the Middle East, and the Ottoman Bank. In the west, Sheikh Khalid's villas were under construction in the area known as "Al Khalidiya".

After a few weeks, I accustomed the life difficulty in Abu Dhabi and liked it, probably because I am of a Bedouin origin and habits, and perhaps because I stayed in an air-conditioned bedroom surrounded by the kindness of my roommate at the old Municipality building facing the sea view on the northern shore. The municipality offices were recently shifted to be adjacent to the Department of Justice in sector W7/01 at Al Khalidiya a few months before my arrival.

Abu Dhabi Municipality Al Khalidiya 1968

Town Planning Section:

In February 1962, H.H Sheikh Shakhbout (RIP) chose Sir William Halcrow Associates and Scott Wilson Kirk Patrick & Partners to submit a field survey report and to prepare a directive plan for the town of Abu Dhabi.

In 1965, Sheikh Shakhbout (RIP) signed an agreement with the Engineering Consultancy Company Arabicon. The ruler selected Arabicon as the Architects to carry out a wide range of works, including the construction of Abu Dhabi Fardha (Jetty), Internal main streets, and Abu Dhabi- Al Ain Road.

In February 1966, Sheikh Shakhbout instructed Messrs. Arabicon to carry out Town Planning tasks and implement three basic projects linking Abu Dhabi to the outside world: Abu Dhabi Airport, Al Maqta bridge, and Harbour.

Arabicon was a British Consultancy Company founded in Abu Dhabi by Messrs. Alan Grant and Associates/Surry England/ Eddie Webb/ Ian Cuthbert. The latter has been appointed as the company's interim representative in Abu Dhabi.

After August 6th 1966, Sheikh Zayed RIP, as the ruler of Abu Dhabi Emirate, assigned Arabicon as sole consultants of all infrastructure projects, including roads, water pipelines, public houses, markets, hospitals, schools, and the Corniche Wall, at the cost of £15 million. Arabicon almost became the sole consultant for infrastructure projects on the island of Abu Dhabi.

Eddie Webb, The Architect and Town Planner asked his colleague Architect John Elliot to work out a modified plan of Abu Dhabi so that the roads would be straight and grid-like the Pakistani city of Lahore, which was visited and liked by Sheikh Zayed, but the Arabicon office in Abu Dhabi was unable, because of the shortage of manpower and technical capabilities, to accomplish such general and detailed plan maps. Thus the job was completed in the London office within 8 months. Drawings and reports were sent to Abu Dhabi by air.

In 1966, an Arabicon equipped office was opened in Abu Dhabi, and the Architect Ken Mitchell was transferred from Lahore to head the

Department of Architecture and Town Planning at the Arabicon office in Abu Dhabi.

Architect John Elliott arrived in Abu Dhabi from London to help his colleague Ken on June 14th 1967, but Ken soon joined Abu Dhabi Municipality and resigned from Arabicon's office. So architect John Elliott became the Director of the Department of Architecture and Planning at Arabicon's office in Abu Dhabi.

In late 1967, Sheikh Zayed decided to run Abu Dhabi Town Planning under governmental supervision as a municipality section. H.H offered architect John Elliott to join Abu Dhabi municipality as Town Planning Director, but the latter apologised because he was busy finalising the designs of the public houses and Abu Dhabi Central Market.

Sunni Banaga, the Director of Abu Dhabi Municipality, announced, in the Lebanese and foreign newspapers, the vacancy of Architect and Town Planner job in Abu Dhabi Municipality. The Japanese national architect Katsuhiko Takahashi, a United Nations expert, was selected as the Chief Town Planner. Takahashi (RIP) received the necessary instructions to perform his duties as government personnel in Abu Dhabi Municipality headed by His Excellency Sheikh Saif bin Mohammed Al Nahyan.

He went to Arabicon's office on his arrival to examine the plans and hand over the drawings from Arabicon office, but Arabicon's Manager, the architect John Elliot, asked him an official letter, especially there were due invoices unpaid. Takahashi returned back to his office, which was a small room attached to the building of Abu Dhabi Municipality.

The basic goal of Mr. Takahashi and his Japanese colleague Mr Tomihara was based on:

a)   A coloured map for land use.

b)   A circulation and traffic skeleton plan.

c)   A zoning plan (East and West Sector division numbering scheme), where the Airport Road is the main Axis.

In late 1968, Arabicon lost control and ability to manage the many projects assigned to by the Ruler because of fatal construction errors that led to the partial collapse of the sea wall of the Corniche and defects in paving materials and street paving. Most projects have thus ceased. This led to the liquidation of the company and the departure of the residing architects to Spain and London after having spent in the desert difficult hot times.

(Info Source: Planning Abu Dhabi. An amazing Urban History narrated by an urban planning specialist / Alamira Reem Bani Hashim).

Town Planning Department:

Dr. Makhlouf Director of Town Planning Department

The Town Planning Department was formed from several sections, namely the planning section, the services section, the section of studies and research, the design section, the building permits section, the land section, the administrative affairs section, the accounts section and the follow-up section, all of which were formed and run by Dr Abdul Rahman Makhlouf, director of the Town Planning Department (1968-1976).

The planning section was the backbone of the department. It was headed efficiently by Engineer Sami Al-Dasher (1969-2004), who was responsible for planning and preparing general and detailed plans for new or replanned areas to develop and meet the needs of the Inhabitants services and facilities.

The planning section also carried out its role in coordination with other sections after the approval of the plans that have been approved and the notification of all service agencies to do the necessary services according to the plans developed.

H.H Sheikh Zayed, Dr Makhlouf, and Samy El Dasher Head of Planning Section 1973

The planning section followed up the development of villages scattered along the roads Abu Dhabi-Al Ain, Abu Dhabi-Dubai and Abu Dhabi-Tarif, and the cities of the western region (now Al Dhafra) and the islands of the Emirate of Abu Dhabi.

The section has continuously created and updated the originals of maps and charts with different graphic metrics. Planning Section supervised the work of surveyors by organising a timetable for fixing sites of public and government buildings. In addition to participation in several technical committees such as the Traffic and Traffic Committee, the Services Committee and the High Committee for Sanitation, Street naming, the audit of GIS databases and aerial photography.

This photo shows His Highness Sheikh Zayed, H.E Buti Al Otaiba
Chairman of AD Municipality, HE Dr Abdul Rahman Makhlouf,
Director of Town Planning Department, and Eng. Samy El Dasher,
Head of the Planning Section, and Dr Dawood Al Rajhi, and Eng. Azmi
Abu Taleb Head of Al Ain Planning Section.

The section also managed a technical archive of the planning database and archiving of the charts, and the preservation of documents with a special archive for the section.

Members of my TPD family, from right to left-back row: The Late Kamel Dakka, Farouq Jamil, Saeed Al Shaer, The late Mr Mirza Rasheed, Mr Azmi Abu Taleb, the Late Eng. Sami Yahya, Dr. Dawood Al Rajhi, and Mohammed Omer. From right to left front row: Assad El Abbas, Ibrahim Badawi, The Late Abdulateef Uthman together with our colleague.

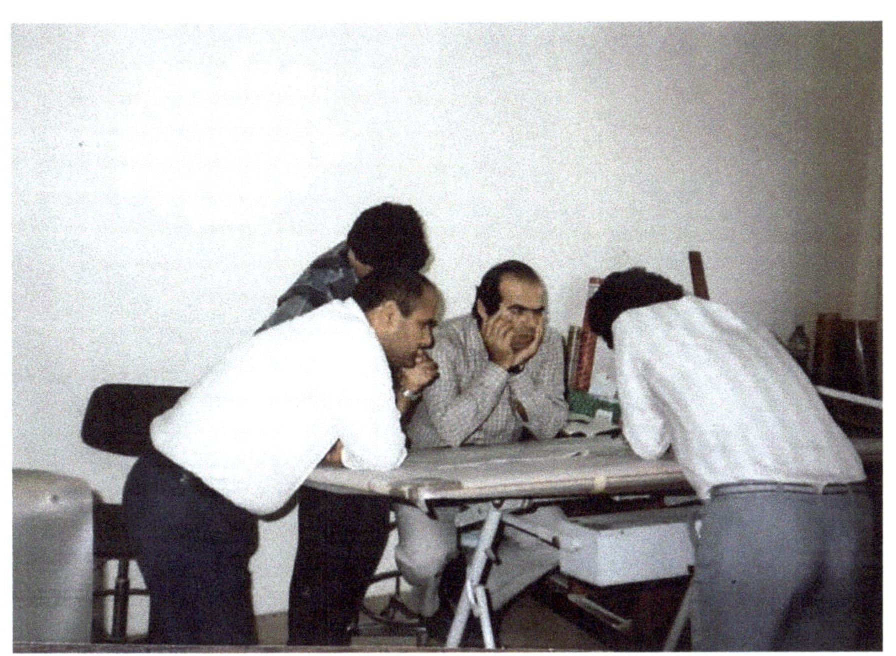

From Left to Right: The Late Adel Azzazi RIP, Adeeb Dhaher, The Late Kamel Daka, and Myself.

Abu Dhabi Town Planning Drawing hall with hand-made drawing tables, long T-squares, set squares, calc transparent paper rolls, Pelican ink bottles, ink erasers, blades, Graphos drawing pens in 1968-1974. God bless those dear gone and long, happy life for those who are still alive!

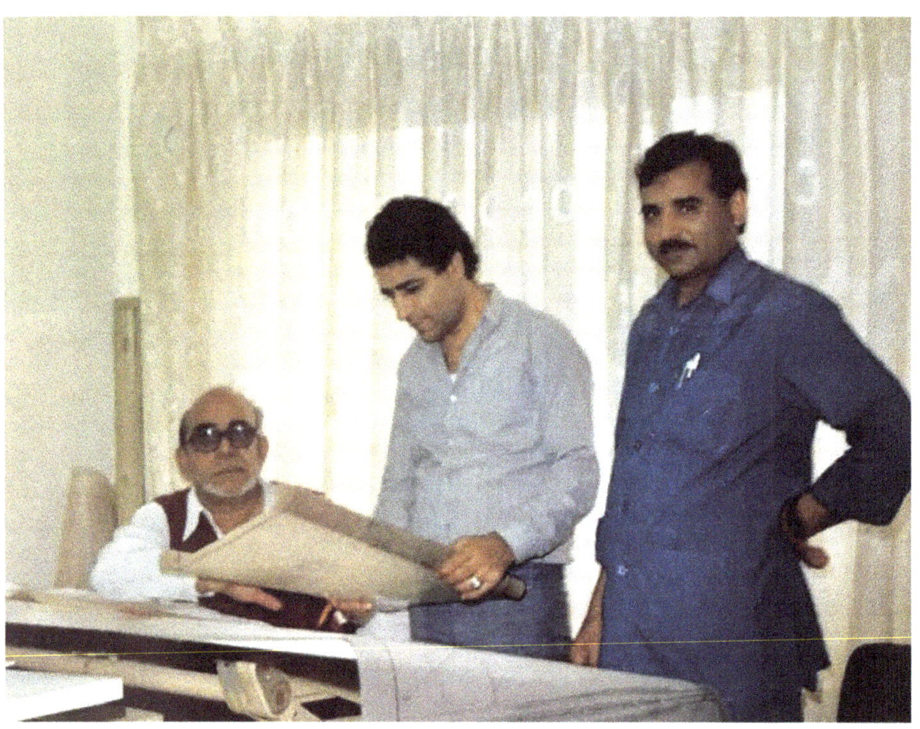

The Author, Head of the Drawing Unit) with the Late Haji Mirza Beig.

Land Management System (LMS):

The purpose of the land management system is to link land types and their uses to meet the needs of developers in the public and private sectors, creating, updating and sharing detailed and public data. In addition, it helps real estate offices analyse and evaluate real estate prices in addition to registering land and extracting site plans and other digital transactions.

GIS Digital Output Showing the Land Use in colour

The number of each plot is linked to a sector number specified by the Town Planning Sector so that each number does not repeat in one sector. The union of the sector number and the plot number are not repeated either.

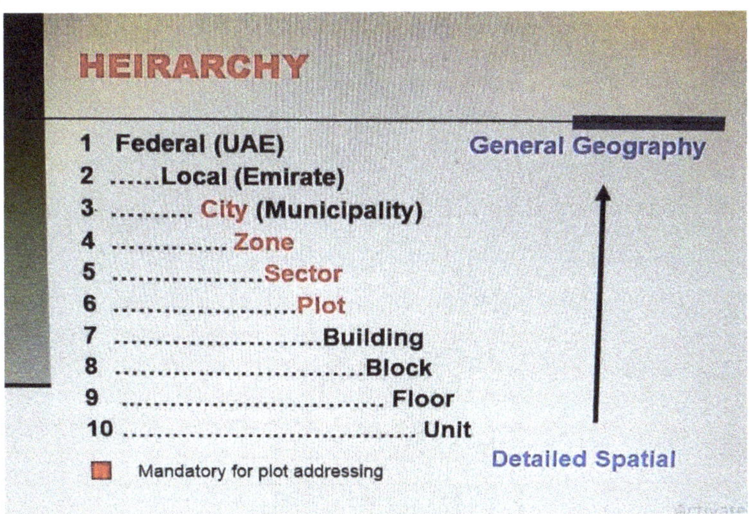

The property hierarchy begins from the residential unit, floor, building, plot of land, sector, area, city, Emirate, state.

Approximately 7 types of land use, including residential, commercial, industrial, public utilities, open space and recreational, infrastructure, agriculture etc., together form a map of land use in the internationally accepted colours for each use!

Many outstanding personalities followed. Each of them carried out his responsibilities towards his people, country, and leadership to the fullest satisfaction.

Department of Planning & Coordination:

Planning Department, other than Town Planning Department. As per the Amiri Decree No. 9 of 1967, Mr Mahmoud Hassan Juma was appointed as the General Manager for Planning and Coordination to make recommendations to His Highness the Ruler regarding the administrative organisation and economic and social development.

Also, coordinating the annual curricula follows up the implementation in the other departments. It gives recommendations to the Ruler regarding laws and regulations concerning personnel and employees appointment affairs.

Department of Information and Tourism:

In 1952, the Kuwaiti Mubarak Al-Mayal broadcasted (Hona Al Kuwait) to be heard for the first time. The Palestinian Mohammed Tawfiq Al Ghussain was appointed to manage the Kuwaiti Radio Station, assisted by Mr Gharbieh. Both gained media experience in the Near East radio station in Cyprus.

In the early 1960s, the inhabitants of the Trucial States heard Cairo Radio and Sawt Al Arab with difficulty, but the radio "Hona London" was overwhelming. Broadcasters were pronouncing Abu Dhabi like "Abu Zabi".

In 1967, with the arrival of the transistor in the Gulf area, people listened to "Sawt Al Sahel" in the Trucial States through the voice of the Palestinian broadcaster Riad Al-Shuaiheen.

On August 1st, 1968, Sheikh Zayed (RIP) issued Circular No. 37 appointing Mr Mohammed Tawfiq Al Ghusain, director-general of the Department of Information and Tourism in Abu Dhabi.

Abu Dhabi in the 1960s became the city where unity sparked out and hopes rose. The Department of Information and Tourism, managed by Mr Al Ghusein, founded Abu Dhabi Broadcasting Station in 1968. On March 5th 1969, Mr Charles Ian Kennedy was appointed as ADBS chief engineer.

During his visit to Great Britain, H.H Sheikh Zayed Bin Sultan Al Nahyan, ruler of Abu Dhabi Emirate, met Lord Thomson, who had already built 37 Radio and TV stations at that time. Abu Dhabi TV Station was created in Abu Dhabi in 1969 and was No. 38 universally.

Four of Thomson's qualified engineers arrived in Abu Dhabi for that purpose and were accommodated at Beach Hotel, at the East side of Abu Dhabi Corniche. The Project Manager was Mr Kiss Danforth and Technical Director Mr Watson. A huge antenna was fixed at the top of Sheikh Suroor Building on Hamdan Street, where the TV Studios and offices exist.

The inauguration of Abu Dhabi TV was in August 1969 by His Highness Sheikh Khalifa Bin Zayed, the Crown Prince at that time. We started to hear the Palestinian Emirati Mr. Khalil Ailabouna's and Palestinian Emirati Mr. Mohammed Al Kodsi's amazing programs and reports.

On October 20th 1969, the publication of Al Ittihad Newspaper in Abu Dhabi followed, where it was printed in Beirut to arrive by air on a weekly basis.

Department of Civil Aviation:

The civil aviation agreements date succeeded the 1935 Military Landing Agreement on Sir Bani Yas Island for 12 years and the subsequent agreements of 1959 and 1962 between Sheikh Shakhbout Bin Sultan (RIP) and Great Britain. The agreements provided the establishment of a runway on Abu Dhabi Island. They provided that all foreigners were allowed to enter Abu Dhabi Island after getting permission from the Ruler's Diwan.

Sheikh Shakhbut Bin Sultan asked the British to improve the Airport infrastructure, which was a landing airstrip and temporary caravans. 1959 agreement stipulated the negotiations with foreign airlines were the prerogative of the mandate government, as an external matter in accordance with the Permanent Peace Agreement. Negotiations included Gulf Air, British Airways BOAC, the Middle East and the operating oil companies.

The Civil Aviation Agreement with Britain in 1962 was the cornerstone of Abu Dhabi's entry into the civil aviation system. But in early 1968, Sheikh Zayed, as Ruler of Abu Dhabi Emirate, concluded a civil aviation agreement with the British that included the operation of an international airport in Abu Dhabi, with permits to fly over Abu Dhabi and land in Abu Dhabi exempted from customs duties.

When Sheikh Zayed Bin Sultan Al Nahyan (RIP) became the Ruler of Abu Dhabi, he focused on connecting Abu Dhabi with its regional and international countries by constructing an international airport. Thus an agreement between the Government of Abu Dhabi and the British Government was signed on January 19, 1967, stating that the British Government will advise on the establishment, maintenance and operation of airports in Abu Dhabi, the maintenance and operation of ancillary facilities, and appointing responsible persons with powers and duties in relation to air navigation and its organisation. (Friday Gulf supplement).

Thus, the Civil Aviation Department was established on January 1st, 1968, to implement aviation affairs, establish airports, apply air transport rules, provisions and agreements, and manage technical and administrative services.

MEA aircraft at Al Bateen Runway on 6th August 1967

The construction of Al Bateen Airport began in May 1966, and the runway was ready to receive the first aircraft on August 6th, 1967. So the first Middle East Airline jet landed, and four companies then operated regular flights, namely Kuwait Airways, Royal Jordanian, Gulf Air and British Airways. Al Bateen Airport continued to operate efficiently until the opening of Abu Dhabi International Airport outside the island in 1982.

In 1973, 4 Gulf States, Bahrain, Qatar, Oman and Abu Dhabi, decided to buy Gulf Air at 25% share each. The company was registered in the first month of 1974 to work as Gulf Air before emerging Dubai's Emirates and Abu Dhabi's Etihad Airways. Later, Al Bateen airport was demolished. Thus the city lost one of its main landmarks of an urban development renaissance.

Source: Fatima Al Mansouri/Zayed Center for Studies and Research

Department of Public Works:

This department, chaired by Sheikh Hamdan Bin Mohammed (RIP), managed the infrastructure development of all aspects, among which Sewerage and Telecommunications.

A.   Abu Dhabi Sewerage:

Messrs. Brian Kolkhoun and associates designed a low-capacity sewerage system on Abu Dhabi Island to serve 30,000 people by constructing two major pumping stations (1 and 2) in sector E28 in 1973. In addition, 22 sub-pumping stations and a network of asbestos pipes with a low-inclination level were in place. With the rapid growth of the city and the ever-increasing population, the station was soon unable to deal with the quantities of sewage it had received.

An emergency committee was formed to cope with the situation and protect the population from contamination, which caused the spread of typhoid fever, ParasotIld, Desantaria, hepatitis, and malaria. The

Committee submitted its recommendations to the Executive Council in 1974, where the government-appointed Messrs. John Taylor and sons (currently Hyder consultancy) developed a plan to meet the city's needs until 1995.

The consultant's mission in designing and constructing expansions to solve limited capacity problems was summarised to the existing purification plant and to connect the various buildings to the sewage network and dispense the analysis tanks the use of treated water in irrigating crops. Today Abu Dhabi's giant STEP sewage tunnel and a 100-meter deep sewage pumping station is fit for the next 100 years in the al-Wathba area.

<u>Telephone and Telegraph:</u>

Abu Dhabi Telegraph and Telephone Company Ltd.

شركة تلغراف و تلفون ابوظبي المحدودة
Abu Dhabi Telegraph & Telephone Co. Ltd.

NOTE - This Telegram cannot be sent unless the declaration at the foot of the Telegram is filled in and signed by the sender. Please write in Block Letters.

TO   ASAA'D HUSSAIN EL ABBAS
RASHIDIA REFUGEE CAMP
SOUR LEBANON

EMPLOYMENT APPROVED EXPECT VISA AND TICKET SOON

TOWN PLANNER

I hereby declare that the text of the above telegram is entirely in plain Language and that it is written in accordance with the general usage of the language.

SIGNATURE & ADDRESS OF SENDER   Abu Dhabi Municipality.
(Not to be Telegraphed)

Job Offer Telegraphed by Mr. Takahashi on 25th January 1968

On December 4, 1961, the telegraph and telephone Office was opened in Abu Dhabi. Since its opening, the office has been serving merchants of Arab and foreign nationalities, which began arriving in Abu Dhabi after announcing the discovery of oil in the Emirate. It had been surface mail before, which took 15 days to arrive on board of East India Company ships.

Abu Dhabi Telegraph and Telephone Company was managed by IAL. IAL constructed huge navigation and transmission towers in Abu Dhabi and Saadiyat Islands. One at Al Khubirat, another at Al Bateen. There was a big camp for IAL at Al Bateen to the south side of the sand dune water tank. IAL moved from ADTT to Emirtel and from Emirtel to Etisalat, where some professionals joined ADTT for 40 years and more. Among the Professionals who installed the network in the latest Etisalat tower on Rashid Bin Saeed Street was Mr. Ken Povall, Dennis Lader, and John Simpson.

I remember that telegram Mr. Takahashi's the chief Town Planner invited me to work in the planning section of the municipality sent from Telegraph and Abu Dhabi Telephone Co., Ltd. (ADTT) on January 25th, 1968.

In late 1962, British telecommunications company Air Radio, which began operating in Sharjah and Dubai, imported phones to Abu Dhabi to install the first telephone network. After it made plans to install 100 telephones in 1962, it began its services at the Governor's Palace and Abu Dhabi City Hall. Due to the growing demand, participants, especially traders, were notified to wait for the survey results to be conducted around Abu Dhabi Island at that time.

Businessman Mohammed Abdul Jalil al-Fahim says as a young eyewitness that the company was founded in 1961, but in contrast with Sheikh Shakhbut RIP, the network, which was proposed from 70 lines to serve oil companies, the British Accreditation House and important sites in Abu Dhabi, was delayed until the dispute was settled in the summer of 1963.

IAL radio tower was seen in 1969. IAL is the company on which it relied and had wireless communication towers in the al-Manaseer area to the north of Abu Dhabi High School. It played an excellent role in establishing and operating Abu Dhabi National Telecommunications Company, which later changed its logo and name and became the giant Etisalat!

B.   <u>**Building Construction Projects 1970-2010:**</u>

1970-1979 Projects:

1.   The work of the new airport

2.   Abu Dhabi General Hospital.

3.   Conference City.

4.   Media Complex.

5.   Zayed Sports City.

1980-1982 Projects:

1.   Al Jazeera Club

2.   The work of the new airport

3.   Dhabi General Hospital.

4.   Conference City.

5.   Media Complex.

6.   Al Ain General Hospital.

Zayed Sports City.

1983-1988 Projects:

1.   Al Jazeera Club

2.   The first stage of Zayed Sports City

3.   Public Library and Cultural Foundation in Abu Dhabi.

4.   Abu Dhabi International Airport infrastructure.

1989-1998 Projects:

1.   New central market and gold and jewellery market

2.   A group of schools for boys and girls in Abu Dhabi

3.   845 popular houses in Bahiya, Al-Dhafra, Al Nahda and Ghayathi

4.   Construction of 16 schools in different locations in Abu Dhabi

1999-2010 Projects:

1.   Construction of 1005 public houses in different areas,

2.   Khalifa Bin Zayed Hospital

3.   Construction of 582 public houses in the areas of Al-Rahba, Al-Shahmah, Al Shamkha and Bani Yas, Al Samha and Al Showaib and Al Wathba.

4.   Sheikh Zayed Bin Sultan II Mosque

5.   Contracting / Khalifa Park in Greater Abu Dhabi City East

6.   Statistics Centre: Development Emirate of Abu Dhabi.

Chapter 7: On The Desert's Dunes

Wilfred Thesiger:

Wilfred Thesiger (Mubarak bin London) Desert Majeure, owner of historical photos of Liwa sands, Empty Quarter (Al Roba Al Khali) and Arabian ranches.

Edward Henderson:

Edward Henderson RIP, born in 1917, arrived from Palestine via Iraq oil company (IPC) and joined Petroleum Development (Trucial Coast) Ltd. Company. In 1959 became full member of Foreign Service and political officer. Edward Henderson wrote confidential reports, descriptive but accurate in their information. We do appreciate this type of report writings and photograph images that have monitored the historical milestones of Abu Dhabi and the UAE at the stage before the declaration of Independence. He was a close friend of Sheikh Zayed Bin Sultan, the Ruler of Abu Dhabi and UAE President. In 1974 he retired from British services and returned back with his wife to Abu Dhabi. He loved Abu Dhabi and worked for the National Centre for Documentation and Research. Mostly, he addressed political situations, administrative and social, economic, demographic, geographical, and living conditions.

His wife Mrs. Jocelyn Henderson, almost 100 years old, arrived Abu Dhabi in 1967, founded the Daly Library, the oldest private library in 1978 carrying Michael Daly's name. She loved Abu Dhabi and UAE and still living in Abu Dhabi since the death of her husband on April 3rd, 1995.

Edward Henderson wrote his Memories of the earlier days in the UAE and Oman titled, From Retreat to Unity.

His remarks about UAE can be singled out. "The union would not have been without sincerity, intention and sincerity to act on their part."

He was impressed by the hospitality enjoyed by the region's people; although they did not have much food and drink. Generosity was the address.

Hugh Boustead:

British Colonel Hugh Boustead, the British Agent in Abu Dhabi (1961-1965).

In February 1962, the Late Sheikh Shakhbut (RIP) was advised by the British Agent Assistant in Abu Dhabi, Sir Hugh Boustead, to invite the Joint Venture of Engineers Halcrow / Scott Wilson Kirk Patrick & Partners, to carry out a study case that includes a Surveying Report and a Directive Plan on blueprints for the island of Abu Dhabi. The report and the directive plan were submitted on time in May 1962.

Mr. Boustead (RIP) was a close friend of Sheikh Zayed. He loved Abu Dhabi and worked for Sheikh Zayed after he retired from British services. Mr. Boustead joined Sheikh Zayed's Horse Stables at Mazyed from 1965 until his death on April 3, 1980.

William Halcrow:

William Halcrow is a famous Town Planner and developer consultant.

In January 1962, Sheikh Shakhbut Bin Sultan Al-Nahyan appointed Sir William Halcrow & Associates and Scott Wilson/Kirk Patrick & Partners, to prepare plans for the development of Abu Dhabi City.

The scheme took into account local customs and traditions and didn't forget the expectation of a higher standard of living and the use of modern techniques.

Based on the population estimates of 25,000, the following projects need to be initiated:

1. Port

2- Power station

3. Seawater desalination plant

4. Road network

5- Airport

6- Hospital

7- Part of the administrative centre

8- Number of 4 residential neighbourhoods

The report pointed the need to organize the government departments to manage and implement the development plan in cooperation with the coalition of engineers concerned.

John Harris:

John Harris, a British national, an architecture and town planning expert who planned the first Dubai city outline in 1960, was the same one with William Halcrow/Scott Wilson Kirk Patrick, the first structural plan for Abu Dhabi and its residential neighbourhoods so that the houses would be directed northward in 1962.

The Pioneer Architect John Harris was involved in community Architectural details.

Typical Residential Neighborhood, Designed by the Famous Godfather of Architectural Consultants of Abu Dhabi, John R Harris.

Tim & Suzan Hillyard:

Tim Hillyard, BP's representative in Abu Dhabi (1956-1960), was 56 years old business expert, a seasoned Arabic-speaking negotiator, a skilled boat pilot between Das Island and Abu Dhabi, and a technician who was maintaining wireless communication systems.

His wife, Mrs Suzan Hillyard, was an amazing woman who lived in Abu Dhabi between 1954 and 1958 and wrote a book entitled (Before Oil)

The Iraq Oil Company (IPC) in Iraq was the starting point for British adventurers seeking wealth in the Trucial Coast. Among them were Mr Tim Hillyard, his wife, Mrs Susan Hillyard, Mrs Honor Cowell, Miss Wanda Jablonski, Mr Roderick Owen, Sir Wilfred Thesiger, Sir Edward Henderson and many others. They were welcomed by senior members of the Royal Family, particularly Sheikh Shakhbut and his close brother Sheikh Zayed Bi Sultan Al Nahyan.

H.H. Sheikha Salama (RIP) used to teach Susan a few words in Arabic every week. The most beautiful greeting she ever heard was that one from her child daughter Deborah who used to say whenever she enters Al Hisn Palace: "Assalam Alaikum (Peace be upon you)" to receive an immediate sheering answer.

Susan Hillyard looks decent and neat in the photo taken by her journalist companion Wanda Jablonski and looks next to Susan, her blonde daughter Deborah, as she shamelessly approaches Sheikh Shakhbut, the Ruler of Abu Dhabi!

Roderic Owen:

Roderic Owen arrived on a small boat to Abu Dhabi, from Bahrain in 1955, as a guest of the B.P. representative in Abu Dhabi, Tim Hillyard, and his wife, Suzan Hillyard.

Tim accompanied his friend to Qasr Al Hisn and presented him as a poet, perhaps because Tim knows that Sheikh Shakhbout and his brothers like poetry. Roderic sat next to H.H Sheikh Shakhbout and his brother Sheikh Khalid after being welcomed, hand shook, and asked: How are you? He replied, "Alhamdulillah."

On the second day, they were invited for lunch, and Roderic brought with him a nice poem saying:

"Through Abu Dhabi's Golden sands

We walked and talked, until the sea

Crept up and disenchanted me

The creeping loneliness of wit,

A future bleak with waves and grit

If there is Hell, oh, this is it!

Oh, this is it, Oh this is it!

Is not all friendship golden sand

We tread together for a while?

Of golden hopes for you and I,

We have so few before we die,

Khalid, so few before we die!"

Poem quoted from:

Shamsa Al Dhahiri Book/A.D. Heritage Club

Wanda Jablonski:

Wanda Jablonski with H.H Sheikh Shakhbout

Wanda Jablonski, a beautiful single blonde oil journalist, has made her way into a male community, born in Czechoslovakia to a botanist father. In 1956 she made a trip to 12 countries in the Middle East.

In January 1957, the American petroleum weekly reporter Wanda arrived in Abu Dhabi to welcome Tim Hillyard and his wife, Susan Hillyard. Tim was B.P.'s representative in Abu Dhabi and director of Adama when it was founded.

During the Arab Oil Conference held in Cairo in 1959, Wanda brought together Saudi Arabia's Representative Abdullah Al-Tarifi with Venezuela's Juan Perez in her room at Cairo Hilton Hotel. The outcome of which was the birth of the Organization of Petroleum Exporting Countries (OPEC).

Wanda arrived at Das Island in 1957 and attended with Tim Hillyard's political representative Pat Townsen. In 1957, B.P. and French Oil Company (Total) completed an oil exploration schedule to take part in Um Al-Chef. An investment of oil project in Das valued at $12 million was established. In 1961, Wanda founded (Petroleum Intelligence) magazine and its first issue were published in January 1963.

Sheikh Shakhbut RIP was described by Wanda Jablonski as follows:

1.   He has a strange intellectual approach.

2.   A religious and humble man.

3.   He has a sense of humour.

4.   His culture is high.

5.   It is not easy to conclude trade agreements with him.

6.   A seasoned negotiator who is a slow mind in his conduct.

7.   He is not prepared to make concessions. He has a high skill in the discussion. He has sharp intelligence, and he doesn't trust those he doesn't know.

8.   Calm nerves even in the darkest crises.

On another occasion, Wanda said:

"Sheikh Shakhbut asked an English political officer:

What is the capital of Nicaragua?

The officer was confused and admitted that he frankly did not know!

Sheikh Shakhbut only told the British political agent that this man of yours is not qualified. He has no familiarity in political geography."

William Round (The Old Brit):

"The Old Brit" nickname was given by Sheikh Zayed (RIP) to the Late William (Bill) Round, the Airport Fire Chief and Fire Safety Advisor during the period (1970_1986) in Abu Dhabi, UAE.

Mr Round arrived in Abu Dhabi in 1970 at the age of 49 after work experience in Africa, Bahrain, and the local Airport of Newcastle, U.K.

He worked hard with the director of Abu Dhabi Airport (Al Bateen Airport) and the Minister of Transportation in 1970 to manage a high standard of Fire Services. Later he was involved in the A.D. Defence Department and fighter jets, air and sea rescue for the helicopters of the oil fields, and once successfully managed firefighting of a ship at Mina Zayed.

Mr Round serviced A.D. Fire Services for 16 years and died on 12/1/2019 at the age of 97 and buried beside his wife, at the same place they married, at Wellingborough, Northamptonshire.

"The Old Brit" with Regret, Rested in peace beside his wife's grave!

Nick Choshrane (Mankabi):

Mr Nick Cochrane-Dyet at Abu Dhabi Book Fair in 2019.

Mr Nick Cochrane-Dyet (Nickname Mankibi) at Hall 12D of Abu Dhabi International Book Fair in 2019. We heard his early days' story in the Emirates. It was a fantastic evening, indeed!

I was lucky to have his signature on a couple of copies of his valuable book, *Early Days in the Emirates*. My host wrote:

"Dear Assad El Abbas,

I am honoured to write this for a true Abu Dhabi expert. I really enjoy your comments & insight.

Sincere thanks & good health,

Nick (مْنْاكبي)

I consider his script and signature as a valuable certificate of honour and priceless gift.

By the way, Mankibi (نگاكبي) is an Arabic word that means, "Head" used as a description of the person mounting responsibilities carefully. That is the nickname given from Sheikh Zayed RIP, to Nick who carried heavy loads of responsibilities since his tender years at Abu Dhabi and Mazyed Royal Horse Stables, UAE.

Chapter 8: Earlier British Activities In The Trucial States

First Coastal Survey of Trucial States:

In 1820, the two survey ships, discovery and Sayki led by Philip Mugan, took off from Bombay British base to the western coast of Musandam, and in 1821, an order was issued to support the survey processing.

In November 1821, Captain Mogan was replaced by his fellow British captain guy, accompanied by Captain Brooks. They continued their mission up to the Qatari border.

On December 1822, the two ships docked in Delma Port to monitor the area between Sir Bani Yas and Khor Al- Obaid.

In 1823, Abu Dhabi, Dalma and neighbouring islands were surveyed. Captain Brooks received help from Sheikh Tahnoon bin Shakhboot (1818-1832), including two boats, two Nokhathas, and a group of guards supervised by his nephew, to secure the survey teams.

In 1824, Surveyor Whitelock surveyed the coast of Abu Dhabi and stated that the discovery research ship crashed near the coast.

In 1825, Captain Brooks completed the survey work of the Arabian Gulf coast and set off to the coast of Persia.

The results of the Abu Dhabi Coast survey says that:

"Abu Dhabi coast from Ras Ghanada East to Al Odaid West is very rich in arrogance.

There are no ports or marinas for large vessels. Arid, barren areas except for some wild herbs, non-populated areas, but visited by Bedouins working in Diving and Fishing seasons".

Quoteation: Abu Dhabi Studies of Social History

Shamsa Hamad Al Dhahiri/ ADHC

British Political Agency:

The British political agency in Abu Dhabi had a prominent management role in the Emirate of Abu Dhabi and the Trucial states prior to 1968 and Independence Day in 1971. In 1955 Sheikh Shakhbout, Ruler of Abu Dhabi Emirate granted the British Political Agency 1.25 acres site besides the seashore. The British thought to import prefabricated bungalows, but later decided to build a two storey building to accommodate the employees in the first floor and the agency offices in the ground floor as well as car sheds. The building was completed in 1956.

The British political agency in Abu Dhabi 1957

By signing the General Peace Treaty, the British Political Resident Mac Loyd proposed the local agent (national agent) position representing the link between the British and the Sheikhdoms in Sharjah, especially the Trucial Coast, was already surveyed and reported.

British Agents:

1954: British Agency opened in Dubai

1954: Assistant to the Political Agent in Abu Dhabi

1955-1958: Assistant Political Agent Martin Buckmaster

1958-1959: Edric Roland Worsnop Assistant Political Agent

1959-1961: Assistant Political Agent Edward Henderson

1961-1965: Hugh Boustead, Political Agent in Abu Dhabi

1965-1968: Archie Lamb, Political Agent, Abu Dhabi

1968-1971: Political Agent in Abu Dhabi Mr H. Treadwell

National Agents:

1825-1849: Mullah Hussein was appointed as national agent in Sharjah

1866-1890: Abdul Rahman Mohammed Al-Serkal, national agent.

1890-1919: Haji Abdul Latif Al-Serkal national gent

1919-1935: Issa AbdulLatif Al-Serkal national agent

1935-1936: Hussein Imad Khansahib national agent

1936-1945: Abdul Razzaq Al-Mahmoud, national agent

1945-1949: Jassim al-Kazmawi, last national agent where the post was abolished in Al Sharjah.

<u>The Saint Joseph's Church:</u>

Saint Joseph Church in Abu Dhabi 1965

Saint Joseph Church was the first church built in Abu Dhabi Island on the land granted by the Ruler of Abu Dhabi, H.H Sheikh Shakhbut Bin Sultan, on June 22nd 1963. Construction of the church began in October 1963. One of the founders was Mr. Michael Daly who arrived in Abu Dhabi in 1958, worked as ADMA vocational training instructor up to 1967 when he started the business as (Daly Trading). The Church was officially inaugurated on February 1965 in the pretence of Bishop Magliacani, though His Highness Sheikh Shakhbut, Ruler of Abu Dhabi

Emirate, and Sheikh Zayed, the Ruler's representative in the eastern region attended the first Christmas celebration held on December 25th 1964.

As the church's location was affected by the Corniche Road project, the church was evacuated and moved on January 1st 1983, to its new headquarters north of the Immigration and Passport Department next to the Mosque of Mohammed bin Zayed Mosque, which name was changed to Maryam Um Issa Mosque. The old St. Joseph on the Corniche was demolished on February 19, 1983.

British Consultants and Contractors in the Trucial States (Samples only):

- John R. Harris and Partners
- Bernard Sunley and Sons
- Costain International Ltd
- Jan Bienkowski
- Neuhaus and Taylor
- Blakedown Landscapes (overseas) Ltd.
- Brashier Lancaster Associates.
- The British Bank of the Middle East
- Cagdas Associates
- Farmer & Dark
- Fitzroy Robinson & Partners
- George, Trew, Dunn, Beckles.
- Willson Bowes.
- Sir Alexander Gibb & Partners.

- Guest, Keen & Nettlefolds.

- Patrick Gwynne.

- Sir William Halcrow & Partners.

- John R Harris Architects.

- Sidney Kaye.

- Firmin & Partners.

- Lloyd's Bank International Ltd.

- Micheal Lyell & Associates.

- Michael Lyell and Partners

- Robert Mathew, Johnson-Marchall & Partners.

- Peddle Thorp Chapman Tylor.

- Percy Thomas & Partnership.

- Precede Cardew & Rider.

- Page and Broughton

- Dubai International Airport was completed in 1971

- Raglan squire & Partners.

- C. Ross & Partners.

- Geoffrey Salmon, Speed Associates.

- Scot, Brownrigg & Turner.

- John Taylor & Sons.

- Abu Dhabi Sewage infrastructure.

- Weightman & Bullen.

- Windell & Trollope

- Wilson Mason & Partners.

- White Young and Partners

Chapter 9: Early Arrivals In Abu Dhabi

Victor Hashim:

From left to right, Sheikh Zayed Bin Sultan RIP, Khalifa Bin Yousef (RIP), Victor Hashim (RIP), and Abdullah Bin Ghanoum (RIP). Around Sheikh Shakhbout RIP in the middle. (National Archive).

Victor Hashim was a French citizen of Lebanese origin. The owner of Atto Company in Bahrain and Abu Dhabi, Trucial states in the 60s. Atto's camp was at the contractor's area E11, Abu Dhabi. He was an active personality, fluent in French and English language. He accompanied the team of arbitration formed in 1951. He was also the representative of the German company, Ziebart, the contractor of Abu Dhabi Central Hospital. The conflict was mediated by the Lebanese Victor Hashim commissioned by Sheikh Shakhbout in 1964-1966.

Emil Al Busstani:

Emil Al-Bustani, owner of the Lebanese company CAT, the company built the Beach Hotel at the current location of Sheraton. The hotel was used by oil companies to accommodate their employees and visitors for short time. The Hotel was managed by a Greek nationality couple named Mr. Carentinos and his wife until 1966.

Dr. Sayed Kurayem:

Dr. Sayed Kurayem, Dean of Arab Architects of the 20th Century.

He was born in the village of Mit Barah, Manufiya, on February 16th, 1911. His father was Minister Engineer Fahmy Kurayem. Sayed studied architecture and graduated from the Faculty of Engineering at Cairo University in 1939, and was ranked the first in the Department of Architecture. Sayed Kurayem got a scholarship to study in Germany where he got his Master's and Doctorate degree in Town Planning from Zurich University.

He became one of the World's famous architects, a UNESCO Town Planning Expert, and a pioneer of modern architecture in the Middle East. He was the owner of Egypt's first consulting office for planning and architecture, he was the first Egyptian to be appointed at the United Nations as a Town Planning Consultant in the 1950s, and was the owner of Egypt's first specialized Magazine of Architecture and Arts in 1939.

Dr. Sayed Kurayem designed some Arab capitals and cities. He has planned more than a few Arab cities, including New Baghdad, New Damascus, Jeddah, Riyadh and Mecca, Khalidiya in Abu Dhabi, and Tangier, Morocco, as well as Greater Cairo cities such as Al Nasr City. He also designed Al Ghargada, on Egypt's Red Sea coast, and also built several historic buildings where he founded Tahrir Square, the Hilton Hotel, the Egyptian Museum, and the Arab League building. He also designed the buildings of famous press organizations such as Today's News, Rose Al Yousef, and Al-Masri.

His work in Abu Dhabi was the planning and design of Khalidiya buildings and its residential villas, Sheikh Khalid buildings on Khalifa Street, the design of the Palace of Al Mushref, Al Manhal Palace, and Al Khalidiya Palace Hotel, at Ras Al-Akhder.

Sheikh Abdulla Faris:

Sheikh Abdullah Faris

Sheikh Abdullah Faris was descended of Nablus. One of the first Arab employees of ADMA worked as a translator in the early days of Abu Dhabi. He was staying at ADMA's villa next to Gray McKenzie at ADMA and ADGAS office complex (now ADNOC) on the corniche. I was friend of Sheikh Abdullah and I used to visit him at his home.

He was a close friend of the late Maad Hashim of Nablus, the brother-in-law of Ali Arab (RIP), the well-known Lebanese politician, the owner of Green Market at the northern entrance of the old Souk, next to the Custom House. We used to buy our daily needs of fresh vegetables that had arrived weekly from Lebanon by air.

The days passed smoothly despite the hot weather. The inhabitants of the city were few and know each other. The percentage of natives among them was above 90%.

Sheikh Abdullah Faris RIP, left after a long time of service and was granted UAE citizenship and a piece of land on which he built a multi-story building on Sheikh Hamdan Street next to al-Yousef Tower. His sons took his role and grew up in their father's footsteps, dedicated to loving the UAE.

Dr. Abdulrahman Makhlouf:

Our beloved TPD Professor Dr. Abdulrahman Makhlouf, Director of Town Planning Department, followed the same way of Dr. Sayed Kurayem. He left for Germany and obtained a PHD degree in Town Planning. He became an expert in Town Planning recognized by the United Nations, designed Arab cities including Cairo, Jeddah, Yanbua, and Abu Dhabi. He opened an engineering office in the same field named "Arab Office For Planning and Architecture" after 8 years spent as Director of Town Planning Department in Abu Dhabi Emirate.

In the photo, Dr. Makhlouf explains to H.H Sheikh Zayed Bin Sultan Al Nahyan (RIP), the Ruler of Abu Dhabi Emirate, the detailed plan and architectural design of the Central Business District (CBD) of Abu Dhabi City.

Al Sunny Banaga:

Director of Abu Dhabi Municipality (1967-1969)

The first director of Abu Dhabi Municipality. Sunny Banagqa was one of three Sudanese appointed by the Sudanese government to the UAE in the 1960s and served as the first director of Abu Dhabi Municipality after Sheikh Zayed RIP, took office.

He was assigned along with Engineer Abdul Shakur Omer Attia, who worked as an official in the road section in late 1966, as well as Mr. Saleh Farah (who served as an advisor of Sheikh Zayed) RIP, and was remarkably active to establish the Department of Justice.

Al Sunny arrived in Abu Dhabi via Beirut and then Bahrain, where there was no direct flights from Khartoum to Abu Dhabi. There were no Sudanese as well, with only two contractors in the UAE, as well as Mr. Kamal Hamza the director of Dubai Municipality.

After arriving in Abu Dhabi, an interview was arranged with Sheikh Zayed at Al Hisn Palace. Sheikh Zayed was a wise man with an insight into the planning of Abu Dhabi city. President Numeiri was the first president to recognise the establishment of the United Arab Emirates, and even the first president to visit the UAE to congratulate the union a few hours after the union declaration. Among those who came to the UAE a few hours later, Taj Al Sirr Hamza, who served as legal adviser at the UAE Ministry of Foreign Affairs.

Mr. Al Sunny proposed to H.H Sheikh Zayed the idea of celebrating the Day of Succession in the form of a military parade. The idea was accepted and it was adopted in 1967.

(*Rakupa info*).

Ahmed Awad Al Karim:

Ahmed Awad al-Karim, Manager of Abu Dhabi Municipality 1975 to 2004.

Ahmed Awad al-Karim, a Sudanese national, served as Manager of Abu Dhabi Municipality from 1975 to 2004. Prior to that, Al Karim has been managing Abu Dhabi Municipality since the beginning of 1968. He has played a major role in the development of Abu Dhabi Cith.

He joined the municipality in January 1968 as an administrative assistant. The Municipality was consisting of basic service sections, including town planning, which was run by a foreign consulting firm

(Arabicon), a waste collection section, a commercial licensing section, and a land registration section. During this period, H.E Sheikh Saif Bin Mohammed Al Nahyan was the Chairmanof the Municipality, followed by H.E Sheikh Tahnoun Bin Mohammed Al Nahyan, and then succeeded H.E Butti Bin Ahmed Al-Otaiba and H.E Khalaf Al Otaiba. In 1975, H.E Sheikh Mohammed Bin Butti Al-Hamed was the Chairman of Abu Dhabi Municipality (1975-2004), Many personnel followed, each of whom fulfilled his responsibilities towards their homeland.

(Info Source: Al Dar News / Al Khaleej Newspaper 25/10/2016)

Dr. Omer Al Khatib:

19/8/1969 Dr. Omer Al Khatib, Director of Abu Dhabi Broadcasting. Based on Emiri Decree No. 31 of 1969, based on what the Chairman of the Department of Information and Tourism H.E Sheikh Ahmed Bin Hamed presented to His Highness the Ruler of Abu Dhabi, Sheikh Zayed issued the appointment of Mr. Omer Al Khatib as Director of Abu Dhabi Broadcasting under the supervision of the Director of the Department of Tourism and Management.

Omer Al-Khatib, born in Palestine 1930, silently passed away on December 7, 2007. The late excelled in "Talk-Show", cultural shows with Arab elite, enriching the hearts of millions of Arab audiences through his interesting programs, which added charm and taste in a special form of his masterful style.

The late held the following positions in Abu Dhabi:

_ Director General of Abu Dhabi Radio and Television (1969-1970).

_Consultant of the UAE Ministry of Information and Culture (1975-1977).

Hanna Elias Khraish:

The Lebanese Contractor Hanna Elias Khraish RIP, owner of Hanna Khraish Contracting Co. witnessed the renaissance of Abu Dhabi.

Building construction started with mud and coral stones, the Lebanese of (Ain Ebel village South Lebanon) Hanna Khreish says:

"I met H.H Sheikh Zayed (RIP) since I came to Abu Dhabi in 1955. H.H helped me in 1959 and iissued me a passport and an exit visa to travel to Kuwait. I remember that H.H Sheikh Zayed RIP was dreaming about Abu Dhabi to be the most beautiful city in the world.

He did achieve his dreams. From the very beginning, he planned and left no time to waste. I remember that the first Sabkha track road in Abu Dhabi was constructed by H.H Sheikh Zayed orders, during the absence of H.H Sheikh Shakhbout RIP.

In 1961, he was saying that Abu Dhabi today is like a two-year-old baby girl, but ten or fifteen years later, she would become a mature pride. Everybody will be fond of her. H.H believed his sense and his dreams come true.

I was the first to enter the concrete block-making machine to Abu Dhabi, the first to get a building permit, and the one who built the oldest Abu Dhabi Municipality building at the Corniche. I got the first license to build an hotel in Abu Dhabi town for Khalifa Bin Hammad.

Most of the workers were from Pakistan pilgrims, who throughout the year stopped during their journey to the Holy Land to perform the Haj."

(Info Source: Al Bayan/from Ibrahim Al Thahali talks.)

Mohammed Mandi:

Calligrapher of the Royals

Mohamed Mandi calligrapher

Mohamed Mandi is one of the most prominent calligraphers in the UAE and the Arab world.

He holds the first calligraphy diploma in the Arab Republic of Egypt in 1977, one of the students of the famous Egyptian calligrapher Sayed Ibrahim, worked for Abu Dhabi Tourism Authority and taught Arabic calligraphy, a member of the Emirates Society of Fine Arts, and participated in internal and external exhibitions.

He held his first personal exhibition at the village of diving and heritage "Habibti Dubai".

He designed the mural of the new Dubai Hospital, has written many amazing Quranic verses in the mosques of UAE and India, and designed the façade of the Court of Ministry of Justice - Abu Dhabi, and the entrance of the Directorate General of Abu Dhabi Police!

He designed the logo of The National Bank of Fujairah, the Abu Dhabi Fishermen's Cooperative Association's logo, the Camel Racing Union's logo, and the logo of the Private Housing Finance Program - Dubai.

He writes Arabic calligraphy in newspapers and magazines, and has a special experience in integrating calligraphy with painting, and has designed many coins for the UAE on many occasions, as well as the UAE currency line (all paper categories), the currency of the State of Bahrain (all paper categories), the currency of the Syrian Arab Republic, UAE passpory, Kuwait, Bahrain, Qatar, and Oman.

Mohamed Mandi is truly an artist and the calligrapher of the royals who deserves our praise and appreciation.

Joseph Dally

Press Photographer

Joseph Dally, a dear friend of mine from Ain Ebel in South Lebanon. I met him at his photography studio at Sheikh Khalid's Building, Khalifa Street, Abu Dhabi in 1968. As a professional press photographer, he trained me how to develop and print photos using diluted acid liquid known as a developer.

Radwan Al Tamimi (Abu Tafish):

The youngman Radwan Osman Al Tamimi

Radwan Osman Al Tamimi fled from his homeland Palestine as a teenager and refuged to Jordan, Syria, Iraq, and boarded to Dubai on a large ship that sailed the distance between Basra and Dubai in four days in 1965.

After arrival in Dubai, he worked at Al Umaraa Restaurant getting 3 rupees a day. After one month he moved to Abu Dhabi to work at «Jerusalem Restaurant" as a waiter getting one Bahraini Dinar a day. When he earned some money he moved to work at Pepsi Cola Factory on the Airport Road as a clerk "Carrany" supervising a driver and two workers to distribute ice cubes for the fishermen at a rate of selling 200 to 300 snowboards daily.

In his spare time, he used to go to the sea shore, opposite Abu Dhabi Hilton. He noticed that there were no water, ice cream, and ice sellers for the passers-by on the corniche. He asked his company to set up a kiosk at the corniche opposite to Hilton Hotel to sell coffee, tea, Pepsi Cola, and water, and it was done.

By God's will, H.H Sheikh Zayed and his three-or-four-car motorcade passed by and stopped because of the people gathering H.H never noticed before.

H.H Sheikh Zayed said: Who's this Kiosk? Someone told him "for this Palestinian-Jordanian".

Radwan went to him and say, "Salam." H.H asked him, "Where are you from?" He answered with a trembling voice, "I am a Palestinian refugee expelled and "Tafashet" from Palestine, to Jordan, Iraq, Dubai, to Abu Dhabi." H.H welcomed Radwan and said, "You're Bu Tafesh then" and asked him to construct and expand the Kiosk.

Radwan said, "I am a poor man, I have no money (Bizat)." Sheikh Zayed (RIP) ordered one of his companions to give him 200,000 Indian rupees and ordered to give him free electricity and water connections. H.H ordered "Bu Tafesh" to expand the kiosk and told him I will pass by you after three days to know what happened. Three days later, His Highness came on time, but Bu Tafesh did nothing.

Bu Tafesh said I haven't had enough money (Bizat) to open a restaurant, so H.H ordered to give him a sum similar to the previous amount that he got.

Thus Bu Tafesh opened the "Sindbad Marine Restaurant and Casino" and ran it for 5 years until the restaurant was affected by the Corniche Road extension, this moved to an area between the Khalidiya Palace Hotel and the Jetty of H.E Sheikh Hamdan Bin Mohammed, under the name of "Golden Beach Restaurant".

Bu Tafesh asked H.H Sheikh Zayed, RIP to set up a Floating Tourist Restaurant, thus giving him enough money to set up the Floating Restaurant and giving him a license to build the ship's restaurant in Al-Bateen Marina which stayed there until 2005.

Bu Tafesh left the place at the request of development authorities, the reason he opened with his sons the restaurant "Bu Tafesh" on Hamdan Street, Tourist Club Area (Al Zahia), Abu Dhabi. 2nd branch opened in Dubai Jumeirah, 3rd branch at al-Bawadi Mall in Al Ain, 4th branch at Khalifa City, Abu Dhabi, and the 5th branch at Al Bateen Marina, Abu Dhabi

The restaurant has become a VIP meeting place in Abu Dhabi, and Ridwan 81 years old now is known by his nickname given to him by the Late Sheikh Zayed (RIP). He used to give nicknames to his beloved persons like "Mankabi" of Nick Cochrane-Dyet and "The Old Brit" of the Late William (Bill) Round RIP.

Chapter 10: Abu Dhabi Amazing Architecture

Octagonal Building, Abu Dhabi Corniche:

This amazing octagonal apartment building is one of two similar designs was to the East side of ADCO complex at Al Khalidiya, besides the oldest church on Abu Dhabi Corniche. This beautiful building was designed by the Egyptian architect Dr. Sayed Kurayem and constructed in 1969.

ADMA Office Building:

The building of ADMA, formed by BP of Britain and Total, was on the ground floor of the old building, and behind it were the two buildings similar to Sheikh Khalid Bin Sultan RIP, designed by Egyptian architect Dr. Sayed Kurayem, on Sheikh Khalifa bin Zayed I Street (formerly Khalifa Street), Abu Dhabi!

Mohamed Harib Al Otaiba Building:

Mohamed Harib Al Otaiba Building, Hamdan Street

The historic building of the first generation on Hamdan Street, Abu Dhabi was designed by the Egyptian Architect Dr. Jalal Mumen. This building is a heritage distinguished by its beauty and simplicity of the architectural design, as the British architect Norman Foster derived from it the exterior elements of the World Trade Mall.

ADNOC Residential Complex:

ADNOC's distinctive residential complex

ADNOC's distinctive residential complex, on Corniche Street near the previous Abu Dhabi Hilton Hotel (Radisson Hotel Now), was built in 1981 with the Corniche club, theatre, cinema, a distinctive restaurant, and gym.

Al Omeira Building:

Al Omeira Building, Hamdan Street, Abu Dhabi

(Al-Omeira building) with a special architectural flavor designed by the Egyptian architect Dr. Farouk Al-Jawhari.

Al Kalily Building:

Al Kalily Building, Zayed The First Street (Electra) Abu Dhabi

The Egyptian Architect Dr. Farouq Al Jawhari's Architectural Masterpiece Al Ibrahimi Restaurant Building, Zayed the 1st Street (Electra Street), Abu Dhabi.

Mariam Bint Sultan Building:

Sheikha Mariam Bint Sultan Building, Hamdan Street

Sheikha Mariam Bint Sultan RIP, sister of His Highness Sheikh Zayed Bin Sultan, a building designed by the Syrian Consultant (SYRCOSULT) was built in 1981 by Al Nasr General Contracting Company.

Hamed Center:

Rear View of Hamed Center, on Zayed the First Street (Electra Street), Abu Dhabi.

This Center was designed by the Syrian origin Emirati National Consultant Zaki Al Homsi (RIP), built by Al Ahmadia General Contracting Company.

Cultural Foundation:

Cultural Foundation, Zayed The First Street, Abu Dhabi

Cultural Foundation is located at the South-East corner of Qasr Al Hosn in Abu Dhabi, designed by by British Architect John Harris. The Cultural Foundation was opened by the President of UAE, the late Sheikh Zayed Bin Sultan (RIP) in 1980. It was renovated and opened again in 2020.

Chapter 11: Abu Dhabi Top 5 Mosques

Zayed Bin Sultan Al-Nahyan Mosque:

Sheikh Zayed Bin Sultan Al-Nahyan Mosque

Sheikh Zayed Bin Sultan Al-Nahyan Mosque is an architectural masterpiece ordered by the founder of the UAE, Sheikh Zayed Bin Sultan Al-Nahyan, in 1986. Through an international competition in which 35 countries participated under the supervision of the Department of Public Works' Chairman Sheikh Sultan Bin Zayed (RIP).

Sheikh Zayed and Sheikh Sultan Bin Zayed RIP with Architect Yousef Abdulki

The design was won by the Belgian Arab Office under the management of the distinguished Syrian architect Youssef Abdulki, and other architects, including engineer Bassem Barghuti, Moataz al-Halabi, and Imad Malas, of PWD, participated in the design and development under the supervision of Abu Dhabi Public Works Department.

The mosque was launched in 1996 and completed in 2008 in two distinctive phases

   1.   The construction of the foundations and the concrete structure was completed by the Italian company Razani.

2.   Finishings and interior and exterior decoration work performed by the Cisco-Arab Construction Coalition.

We remember from the engineers of the second phase, Engineer Munther Sultan after the Cisco/Arab Construction Company who began his work after work was stopped for some time in addition to the hundreds of engineers, technicians, and workers who contributed to the construction of this amazing Landmark.

The total area of the site is 500,000 m2, the mosque area is 22,412 square metres, 420 metres long, by 290 metres wide, and 33 metres high.

The mosque has four minarets, each 107 meters high, and the domes number 74 domes, the style of Mughal architecture. The height of the biggest dome is 70 meters high and has a diameter of 32.8 meters. The floor level of the mosque is 9 meters above the level of the road next door. That makes the mosque looks higher to the sight of the coming from far!

Dome Before and After

The photograph, shows the dome literally taken footage of the same place twice: (before and after), during work on the Project, is sourced from "Beno Saradzic" for photography as printed on and is displayed on the Internet.

The photography date shown on the two images refers to the year of the photograph of the concrete structure because the decoration and finishing work took place years later between 2002 and 2008.

The stunning Sheikh Zayed Bin Sultan Mosque was designed as mentioned by the remarkable Syrian architect, Yousef Abdulki. I am proud of his Islamic architecture and culture. Though he is a Christian, his talented brain created this magnificent design of this distinctive Islamic Landmark

The original design of Sheikh Zayed Bin Sultan Mosque

The original design of Sheikh Zayed Bin Sultan Mosque before the amendment of domes' style. The domes were smoothened to avoid the horrible clumsy grooving.

Jungle of palm trees imported by Mr. Abdulki the Architect, while designing the passages of Sheikh Zayed Bin Sultan Grand Mosque in Abu Dhabi. Look at the caps of the columns and compare them with palm tree fronds. Amazing employment of environmental features! The Mosque became a Global Touristic Destination.

The pillars of the Ewan corridors

The pillars of the corridors surrounding the outer courtyard of Sheikh Zayed Bin Sultan Al-Nahyan Mosque accounts 1048 marble-covered columns inlaid with semi-precious stones, floral designs, and colorful flowers, as well as the crowns of the columns tastefully designed by the palm of gilded aluminum.

Our theme is the semi-precious stones that were stacked in the columns of the hallway at Sheikh Zayed's Mosque, inspired by several photos taken by the artist Munther Sultan, supervisor of decoration work within the Cisco/Arab

Construction team, to document the stages of engraving work on white marble and embed it with semi-precious stones.

"This artistic mission was carried out by Saray Indian Company, which was brought from its workshop in India by the finest artisans who are closely related to those who worked in the decoration of the Taj Mahal Mosque, and demonstrated their creations in the masterpiece of Mughal Islamic architecture in India," says Sultan.

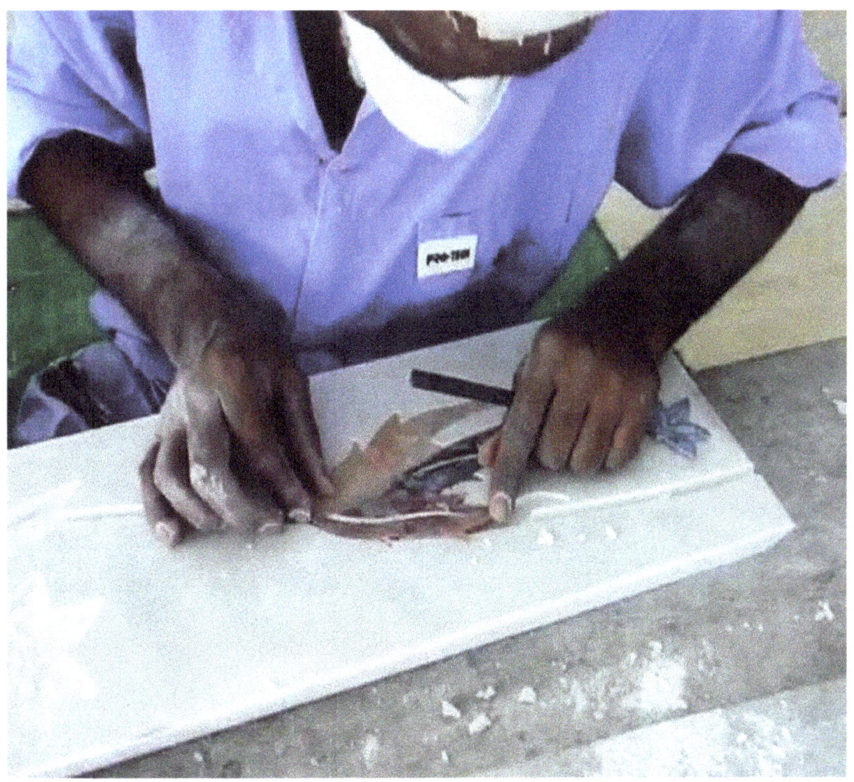

Fixing the Semi Precious Stones

It took about a year and a half for two teams, one in India and the other in Abu Dhabi, to be dug up, fixed, and cleared marble, where the second team planted them inside the marble pieces so that the Turkish contractor Haz Marble would install them on the columns as we see them today."

Semi Precious Stones After Fixing and Rendering

"It is worth mentioning here that the number of semi-precious pieces used in the project is about one million pieces, and the number of columns studded with about 1048 columns, as mentioned above so that the single column included about 1,000 pieces of different shapes, colors, and sizes." As for the flower on the faces of the columns, it is derived from the flower, which was an important source of inspiration in the architectural elements of the Mosque of "Taj Mahal", as if the formation that we see now is a new trend in its depiction of the Indians, especially since the UAE team was in favor of imitating the Taj Mahal, or at the minimum influenced by it, luxury it in a new and attractive way to avoid repetition.

The Largest Persian Carpet Ever

The mosque carpet, an event and nothing wrong, is the largest carpet in the world with an area of 5,700 square meters, which was made by 1,200 hand sewing technicians and took 12 months to work. The carpet consists of four pieces weighing five and a half tons, and the carpet costs $8.5 million. The carpet industry was supervised by more than 50 experts and used 25 colours extracted from traditional herbs and foliage veins. The carpet numbered 2.5 billion knots and was implemented in the eastern Iranian province of Khorasan. It weighed about 45 tons and was transported to Abu Dhabi on two giant planes to combine luxury and quality and to be at the level of this mosque, which bore the name of the beloved of millions Sheikh Zayed Bin Sultan Al Nahyan, founder of the UAE, (RIP).

Zayed the 1st Grand Mosque:

Sheikh Zayed the First Mosque 1970

Its located on Zayed the First Street, opposite the cultural Foundation, south of Qasr Al Hosn. It lies in the area formerly known as "Dairat Al Miah". It was the first grand Mosque for Jumaa prayer with high capacity to be built in Abu Dhabi. It was completed in 1969 by order of the Ruler of Abu Dhabi Emirate, H.H Sheikh Zayed Bin Sultan Al Nahyan RIP. It was designed by the consultants' office of Messrs Zaki Al-Homsi and Hisham Al-Husseini. Architect Hisham Al Husaini was in Abu Dhabi and Structural Engineer Al Homsi in Dubai. They worked together to finalize this grand mosque as soon as possible. Mr. Al Husaini asked me to join his office located at Sheikh Khalid Bin Sultan's Building on Khalifa Street to amend some drawing details on a part-time basis. I was very happy to earn extra money for the preparation of my wedding in the next year 1969.

Sheikh Sultan Bin Zayed The First Mosque:

Sheikh Sultan Bin Zayed The First Old Mosque

One of Abu Dhabi's old mosques was used as Eid prayer in Al Bateen area in the past. It was designed and implemented by the Public Works Department. It was the mosque where Al Janaza prayer was held on the soul of the United Arab Emirates Founder, Sheikh Zayed Bin Sultan Al Nahyan RIP. The mosque has been reconstructed in the local architectural with square-shaped Moroccan style minarets.

Sheikh Sultan Bin Zayed The First New Mosque

Sheikh Sultan Bin Zayed The First New Mosque is facing Khor Al-Bateen in the west sector W35 of Al Bateen area of Abu Dhabi

Khalifa Bin Zayed The 1st Mosque:

Al Otaibat Mosque (Khalaf Mosque) in Abu Dhabi

Al Otaibat Mosque (Khalaf Mosque) in Abu Dhabi was existing to the
north of Qasr Al Hosn opposite the British Agency in Abu Dhabi

(Currently the Sheikh Khalifa Bin Zayed The 1st Mosque). The mosque was previously built of mud, coral stones, and gravel, distinguished by its bold columns and huge circular minaret. The ceiling was made of wood and palm fronds.

The Imam was Abdullah Al-Sayed Al-Hashimi, during the rule of H.H Sheikh Shakhbout and H.H Sheikh Zayed RIP. The Imam succeeded his uncle, who spent many years as imam of the mosque until he lost his sight.

The imam's house was in the past a stone dwelling next to Qasr Al Hosn, where he lived without electricity. When electricity was connected to Qasr Al Hosn H.H Sheikh Shakhbout RIP, ordered to connect electricity to the Imam's house.

Sheikh Khalifa Bin Zayed The First mosque in Abu Dhabi.

One of the oldest mosques of the late 1970s designed by the Town Planning Department under the management of Dr. Abdulrahman Makhlouf. It was designed by the talented TPD Egyptian Architect / Dr. Dawoud Al Rajhi.

The mosque was built in 1979-1981 instead of the old historical Al Otaibat mosque, opposite the British embassy, on Al Hosn Street, (Khalid Bin Al Waleed, formerly), to accommodate about 2000 prayers.

It was designed in a rectangular shape, with eight domes and two minarets similar to the Ottoman Architecture style. The major domes are three, the biggest dome and two smaller ones of Ottoman-style also.

Mariam Um Eisa Mosque (PBUT):

Mariam Um Eisa Mosque (PBUT)

The inside columns are octagonal with marble finishing, and the walls and the inner domes were decorated in such a way that made the mosque an exquisite masterpiece.

Previous name (Sheikh Mohammed Bin Zayed Mosque) in the West sector 24/2, north of the Immigration and Passport Department, and adjacent to Abu Dhabi block of churches. The mosque was renamed the (Maryam Um Issa Mosque PBUT) on June 15th, 2017.

It was built in 1985, to have a capacity of 1,500 prayers, has 4 minarets inspired from Ottoman architecture, and features its main dome, surrounded by 32 windows with stained colored glass reflecting the sunlight during the day.

The mosque is adjacent to catholic and Protostant churches and schools practicing worship with harmony and cool environment!

Chapter 12: Abu Dhabi Top 5 Palaces

Qasr Al Hosn:

Qasr Al Hosn is the oldest stone building on Abu Dhabi Island

It was originally constructed as a control tower besides the water well discovered on the island by a team of hunters in 1761. Since then it became the headquarter of Sheikhdom of Al Nahyan.The leader of the

Bani Yas Tribes moved from Al-Mariya in Liwa to Abu Dhabi. The inner fort was built by Sheikh Shakhbut Bin Dhiab Al-Nahyan, in 1793 and became the palace of the ruling family.

This landmark, which was on the outskirts of the town and is now in the midst of the capital city, has two important building blocks: The "Inner Fort", which dates back to almost 1793-1795, and the "outer Fort" built during 1939-1940. Both represent the vibrant lung and the living witness of Abu Dhabi's history.

Qasr Al Hosn is located between Hamdan Street north and Zayed The First Street south, Sheikh Rashid Bin Saeed Street East and Khalid Bin Al Waleed Street (Al-Hosn Street) west,

On the occasion of the first oil exploration concession in AD Emirate in 1939, the outer fort was built more similar to the old fort. Al Hosn remained a Royal Family palace until the completion of the construction of Al Manhal Palace, where it became a center of Documentation and Research Department after his Highness Sheikh Zayed Bin Sultan Al-Nahyan moved to Al Manhal Palace and Al Bahr Palace

As we examine the building materials, architectural details, building materials, architectural blocks, domes, towers, boundaries, and window openings as well as the decorations, we inspire the historical power despite the harshness of the weather and difficulties of life in the past.

The majestic Qasr Al Hosn was outs6the town center. To the West of Qasr Al Hosn, was the neighborhood of Al-Maharbah, where the earlier palm frond houses were scattered. To the North, was Sheikh Khalifa Bin Zayed's palace inherited by his only Son Sheikh Mohammed Bin Khalifa

(RIP), the peaceful and wise man who accompanied Sheikh Shakhbout RIP, and Sheikh Zayed RIP, and shoudered Al-Nahyan Family. He strongly supported the position of H.H Sheikh Zayed who brought together the tribes to unite and the Trucial States to cooperate and establish the state of the United Arab Emirates!

Qasr Al Hosn is now located in the city center. Al Hosn comprises the West Sector W3, to form with the Cultural Foundation a Cultural Square.

Qasr Al Hosn recently witnessed a wide range of renovation, maintenance, and restoration works as the most prominent landmark and historical witness that recounts the past of Abu Dhabi Emirate, its beginnings, history, cultural and architectural heritage.

It reminds us of the history of the grandfathers and their ability to build and reconstruct despite the harsh conditions. It reminds us of their traditions and high-quality values over time.

The renovation works carried out at Qasr Al Hosn to preserve the features and prestige of the fort, is of great importance because it offers us a general vision of a historical landmark that has undergone multiple stages of construction and renovation due to its different roles over time.

Such amendments made the history analyst Mr. Paul Woodlock, admin of Abu Dhabi Good Old Days Group says:

"Even Al-Hosn fort isn't original now, but mostly a reconstruction."

Qasr Al Manhal:

Al Manhal Palace, Rashed Bin Saeed Street, Abu Dhabi

Al Manhal Palace, the Diwan of His Highness the Ruler, and the UAE Presidential office in Abu Dhabi after moving from Qasr Al Hosn. It witnessed the event of raising the UAE flag in Abu Dhabi to the first time.

Al Manhal Palace was designed by the Egyptian Architect Sayed Kurayem RIP in 1966_1967. The palace occupies Sector West 4/01, according to the Municipal Sector divisions. To the north of the palace, lies Sheikh Zayed's The First mosque, with two minarets 40 meters high.

After H.H was elected President of UAE, His Highness Sheikh Zayed Bin Sultan Al Nahyan raised the flag of the United Arab Emirates for the first time on the flag pole located at Al Jumeirah Palace in Dubai, where the military fired twenty-one rounds of greeting on the occasion.

Following the announcement of the establishment of the United Arab Emirates, His Highness Sheikh Khalifa Bin Zayed Al Nahyan, the then Prime Minister, went to Al-Manhal Palace Square and raised the UAE flag on Al-Manhal Palace. Two of the Amiri Guard Soldiers raised the flag and His Highness the Crown prince and the Prime Minister paid tribute to the flag of the Federation, which had been fluttered in the country for the first time.

Qasr Al Mushref:

Al Mushref Palace, Al Karama Street, Abu Dhabi

Qasr Al Mushref is an Architectural masterpiece of the 60s. It was designed by the Egyptian Architect Dr. Sayed Kurayem. Besides the palace, there was a camel racing track and a wedding celebration Yard. To the south lies the Hunting and Equestrian Club. While on the east side lies Um Al Emarat Park (Al Mushref Garden previously).

This Palace was the founder, Sheikh Zayed bin Sultan Al-Nahyan's meetings place, where his sons and followers attended the lessons and learn the values, morals, and the relationship between the ruler and his people. It inspired humility and love for the country and the people. Sheikh Khalifa UAE President and H.H Sheikh Mohammed Bin Zayed, Crown Prince, Abu Dhabi de Facto Ruler worked together to achieve pride and dignity, progress and prosperity, innovation and creativity for Abu Dhabi and UAE.

Qasr Al Bahr:

Qasr Al Bahr, Sheikh Zayed Bin Sultan Street

Qasr Al Bahr on the east side of Sheikh Zayed Bin Sultan Main Road. The palace is surrounded by greenery and Al Garm trees covering the sea waters. It is facing Al Reem Island with beautiful scenery and amazing touristic views. The Palace is reached from west to east Main Street crossing Sheikh Zayed Bin Sultan Street named (Fatima Bint Mubarak Street (previously Delma Street). The new name denotes the eternal love and relations between H.H Um Al Emarat and the UAE Founder Sheikh Zayed Bin Sultan Al Nahyan RIP.

Qasr Al Watan:

Qasr Al Watan, Ras Al Akhder, Abu Dhabi

A unique Architectural Masterpiece that embodies the progress of the United Arab Emirates and serves as a bridge for knowledge and civilizational communication among the peoples of the world.

With its lavish corridors, the palace offers you the opportunity to enhance and enrich your experiences, to learn about our wise leadership in building the nation, and their role in preserving and disseminating Arab contributions in various fields of knowledge, as well as shedding light on our rich Arab heritage that reflects our unique identity and privacy.

The palace is a masterpiece of Art and Architecture you wonder as it is open for the republic. The palace corridors are inspired by the authentic Arab tradition and its windows that embody the spirit of the forward-looking nation.

Chapter 13: Abu Dhabi Top 5 Oldest Markets (Souks)

Arabicon Central Market:

Arabicon's Vegetable, Meat, and Fish Markets 1973

Arabicon's Vegetable, Meat, and Fish Markets at the top photo were built in the 1960s. They were designed by the British Architect John Elliott director of the architecture and planning department of Arabicon's Abu Dhabi office. The roof was UK style, with sloppy roofs casting shadows and allowing sunlight.

The markets were demolished and replaced by a parking for the adjacent central market, was finally demolished and replaced by "The Mall" with its 2 skyscrapers of Abu Dhabi World Trade Center (WTC)

Old Central Market:

The old central market designed by the Town Planning Department by The late Egyptian Architect Sami Yahya, managed by Dr. Abdulrahman Makhlouf, Director of Town Planning in the Emirate of Abu Dhabi (1968-1976), separated by Khalifa Street in 1979.

Abu Dhabi Central Market, Abu Dhabi (1970-2005)

Abu Dhabi Central Market was the most preferable public place for shopping in the open air amid the city center. All beautiful memories and popular events are still remembered from the early 1970s. All kind of traditional and modern goods were available in the 1980s and 1990s before its demolition in 2005. AlDar planned the Mall (WTC) the World Trade Center, which combined the old and new markets in one shopping center full of m odernity and privacy amid the CBD of Abu Dhabi Capital City!

Abu Dhabi World Trade Center (WTC)

The latest Mall was designed by the British Consultants Foster & Co., and the implementation of the leading Arab construction company ACC!

We notice that the interest of consultant Foster & Co. in the urban environment and the need for harmony with the adjacent buildings in what is known as Environmental Architecture. He realized the valuable domestic elements of the local architecture of the adjacent Al Otaiba building of the 60s designed by the Egyptian consultant Jalal Momen, for cladding the elevations of the mall completely, as well as all the building blocks in the vicinity of the hanging gardens.

New Central Market:

The New Market, Khalifa Street (Demolished) 1973

The New Market in Sector E1, along with Khalifa Street Abu Dhabi as shown in 1973. To the left, we see Amiri building, Mohammed Rasool Khoury (Rolex Building), and Abdulla Khoury, along Al Ittihad Square. These buildings constructed earlier return to the old Top traders at the start of Abu Dhabi's growth in the 60s. The New market was built in the same site which was occupied by the old souk with narrow lane and covered by rags and tents.

The Old Traditional Souk 1950s (Mustafa Alhindi)

The new market was demolished and replaced by The Mall of Abu Dhabi World Trade Center (WTC)

Vegetables, Meat, Fish & Clothes Market (W2):

Clothes Market (W2) interior Facades

Abu Dhabi W2, Vegetable, Meat, and Fish Souk interior. Unfortunately, these amazing arcs were demolished. How easy to demolish, how difficult to build!

This marvelous market demolished in 2005, and shops shifted to the new vegitable, meat, and fish market to the south of Gold Market at "Madinat Zayed Market" ".

New York University Campus NYU postponed its activity there and shifted to its new campus at Al Sadiyat Island. The UAE Diplomatic Academy took its place near Sheikh Khalifa The First Mosque.

General View of huge Market, Hamdan Street W2

Some of the comments received describing their sorrow to demolish such an extraordinary structure: "Wonderful memories and best fish ever. We were so lucky to live in Abu Dhabi back in the good old times when it was still a real typical Arab Gulf town slowly becoming a city. Now no more landmarks all faceless towers." *(Martina Conrad)*

Partial View of huge Market, Hamdan Street W2

"This was a beautiful building (just like the big Souq by Abdelrahman Makhlouf). An amazing sample of neo vernacular modernist approach with unique brutalist elements. It was a pity to lose. In the meanwhile, the NYUAD campus also moved out in 2014-2015 to its brand new Saadiyat location." *(Apostolos Kyriazis)*.

Just to remind the reader that the old market passed in different phases of developments during the last decades between the 1960s and 1990s.

W2 Market in the 1960s in front of the Police compound

Madinat Zayed Shopping Center:

Madinat Zayed Shopping Center, Sultan bin Zayed The First Street.

Madinat Zayed Shopping Center is located on Sultan bin Zayed The First Street in the heart of Abu Dhabi City. The market includes more than 500 different stores combining the past and the present. It can be divided into three main sections:

a)   A traditional section on the north side of clothing, perfumes, antiques, toys, and electronics, etc.

b)   Gold and diamond jewelry section on the south side.

c)   A section of The Lulu Hypermarket, a variety of sales, international brands, and house needs in the middle.

The market area is 50,000 square meters and the Lulu market has an area of 150,000 square feet. The market's working time lasts between 9:00 a.m. and 12:00 a.m. Saturday to Thursday, as well as the opening of the gold market from 9:00 p.m. to 10:30 p.m. with part-time on Fridays.

The design of the market is characterised by its beauty and modernity, topped with green and blue domes decorated with mosaics, designed by the Town Planning Department of Abu Dhabi Municipality.

The market is one of the oldest traditional and traditional markets for shoppers for more than 30 years at an access rate of 14 million customers per year. Especially, it is very near to the vegetables, fruits, meat, and fish market. The Shopping Center has been managed and operated by Lulu since 2007 and has made expansions and updates combining the northern and southern markets in 2011 with the development of the middle market. The market enjoys a vast parking area and carts trolls to transport shoppers' goods easily.

Chapter 14: Abu Dhabi Top 5 Oldest Hotels

Subhan Allah Hotel:

Subhan Allah Hotel in Abu Dhabi 1961

It was an inn and restaurant of the virtuous man/ Mr. Mohammed Al-Hashimi, the hospitable man and father of Mr. Abdullah Al Sayed Mohammad Al Hashimi.

The owner Sayed Mohammed Al-Hashimi, who since long accompanied the Rulers of Abu Dhabi, was one of the loyal men and followers of Sheikh Shakhbout Bin Sultan Al-Nahyan and Sheikh Zayed Bin Sultan al-Nahyan RIP.

During Sheikh Zayed's life, Al-Hashimi served as his personal companion, then was appointed director of the Private Department, and was the chief financial and administrative officer for construction projects directed by Sheikh Zayed, as well as hajj and umrah projects at Sheikh Zayed's expense.

The Beach Hotel:

The Beach Hotel 1964/65 (Michael Stokes)

By the 1961 agreement between Sheikh Shakhbut Bin Sultan, Ruler of Abu Dhabi RIP, and the (Contracting And Trading) company (CAT), owned by the Lebanese urban developer and construction projects Emil Al-Bustani, to build government buildings furnished for employees, a modern hotel was built at that time (Beach Hotel).

The Beach Hotel was used mostly by the employees of the oil companies, airlines' crew and VIP visitors. The hotel manager until 1966 was the Greek National Mr Carentinos and his wife. The Beach Hotel turned into Abu Dhabi Sheraton Hotel.

Abu Dhabi Sheraton Hotel; Corniche Road

Sheraton Hotel was designed in 1977 by the British Architects: Rothermel Cooke (with John Harris and Sutherland structural Engineers, and Jon Shreeves and Partners as quantity surveyors), 420 rooms, night club, cinema, swimming pool, sauna, and bowling. The outer walls traditional design curtain views towards the main Corniche Road, while

Seaside is open to the gulf sea view. Sheraton opened up for business in the spring of 1979.

Khalidiya Palace Hotel:

Old Khalidiyah Palace Hotel

Khalidiyah Palace Hotel, one of the oldest hotels in Abu Dhabi. It was designed by the Egyptian Architect Dr. Sayed Kurayem to be a palace for H.E Sheikh Khalid Bin Sultan RIP, the elder brother of Sheikh Zayed RIP. It was modified in mid of 1970s to be a hotel under Al Khalidiya Palace Hotel. There was a direct access aggregate sand road between Al

Khalidiya Villas and the palace at the sea tongue in the western part of the island.

This hotel was renovated in the 1980s and the area around it developed where the Presidential Palace was built and greenery spread around. A few years later the old hotel was demolished and high quality 5 stars hotel was reconstructed.

Khalidiya Palace Hotel New

Khalidiya Palace Abu Dhabi is now a premier five-star family resort located at the end of the Corniche Road, at Ras Al Akhder overlooking the Gulf, with 200 long private sea beaches and largest swimming pools, and the Presidential Palace, close to tourist attractions, cultural landmarks, and popular malls.

Al-Ain Palace Hotel:

A great photo of Abu Dhabi Corniche and Old Al Ain Palace Hotel; Corniche Road (Paul Woodlock)

Khalifa Street from east to west filled with beautiful and descripted memories. Qasr Al-Ain Hotel, owned by the late Sheikh Mubarak Bin

Mohammed, the father of His Excellency Sheikh Nahyan Bin Mubarak Al-Nahyan, Minister of Tolerance. Built by the Arab Contracting Company owned by (H.E. Khalaf Al-Otaiba and Engineer Adnan Derbas). The hotel was opened in 1967.

I met Mr. Takahashi, Abu Dhabi Chief Town Planner, while staying at Al Ain Palace Hotel in 1968. The pool behind the hotel opened in 1975. Few steps from the seashore. The hotel manager was at that time the beloved Greek open minded Mr. Mitirio. So many people have many happy hours in the Ally Pally, swimming pool, and variety of food tastes restaurants.

To the left of the photo appears the building of Federal Residence, and to the middle appears ADMA building where were Travel Offices of Gray McKenzie, Next to it the two similar buildings of Sheikh Khalid bin Sultan RIP, designed by the Egyptian Architect Dr. Sayed Kurayem, along Sheikh Khalifa Bin Zayed The 1st Street (Formerly Khalifa Street), Abu Dhabi.

South of the hotel was a BP filling station opposite to ADMA-Opco office building which was built in the 1955. There was also a telephone and telegraph office.

To the east of Al Ain Palace Hotel, there were typical villas for the oil company when ADNOC had not yet been established. To the west of the hotel were ADMA's Villas, one of which was inhabited by Sheikh Abdullah Faris of Nablus. He had worked for oil companies in the Gulf area since 1948.

Gray Mackenzie Complex, Maritime Services, and Travel Office Bureau were established after an agreement with Sheikh Shakhbout in the early 1960s to import heavy machinery and load and download goods in Abu Dhabi's small port (Al-Fardha) in front of Custom House.

The Federal Residence was used by ADMA as a rest house to accommodate its new employees and provide temporary residence between 3 and 6 months before moving into furnished flats. It was also a leisure resort for the field staff to periodically eliminate the effects of gas on their health. A lot of stories can be told about this place we used to pass by or visit in those old days!

Abu Dhabi Hilton Hotel:

Abu Dhabi Hilton (Nawaf Abu Ghazaleh)

Abu Dhabi Hilton is Abu Dhabi's first 5-star luxury 183 upgraded to 221 bedrooms hotel, designed in 1971 by Brashier Consultants, specifically for the hot climate. The exterior remains cool even A/Cs are off. It included a shaded swimming pool on the first floor. The hotel was officially opened in the presence of His Highness Sheikh Zayed bin Sultan Al-Nahyan, President of State, on May 23rd, 1973.

Abu Dhabi Hilton Under Construction (Nawaf Abu Ghazaleh)

Chapter 15: Abu Dhabi Top 5 Oldest Cinemas

BP's – Cinema:

BP's Cinema Screen on the Rear Wall (Mustafa Alhindi)

The oldest cinema screen in the open air in Abu Dhabi was just a white painted wall adjacent to Sheikh Hazza Bin Sultan's house. It was prepared by BP's Representatives to announce oil exploration activities. One of their films was was about oil industry "The New Explorers". Mr Tim Hillyard and his wife Mrs. Suzan tried to educate the inhabitants and encourage them to join BP-Total for better income.

Al Maria Cinema:

Old Al Maria Cinema open to Sky (National Archive)

The Open to Sky Al Maria Cinema in the 60s was the oldest regular cinema in the open air. One could watch the movies from their adjacent flats and Zakher Hotel. The cinema was renovated in the 1980s, demolished and rebuilt in 2000. Al Maria is one of the oldest nonstop cinemas in Abu Dhabi. It had been transformed from an open to sky cinema to a modern one having 9 theatres with around 2100 seats, offering a very high level of entertainment due to the long competitive experience.

New Al Maria Cinema and Mall

Now Al Maria is a giant Mall at Liwa Street, Abu Dhabi, where Al Maria Cinema is part of it.

Al Ferdous Cinema:

Old Al Ferdous Cinema Open To Sky

This open to sky cinema was to the East side of the Beach Hotel (Now Sheraton Abu Dhabi Hotel), which dates back to the 1960s. Abu Dhabi inhabitants at that time mainly were of the male gender. There was an amusement area called among the males as "Sikat Al Khail" in Sector E13.

Sheraton Hotel first opened in 1979-1980 and was renovated in 2002-2003. The photo shows Al Ferdous Cinema and the Sheraton with its memorial monuments at the intersection of Corniche Street and Mina Street.

The National Cinema, Delma Street, Abu Dhabi

The National Cinema is one of the oldest cinemas in Abu Dhabi. I don't remember that the National was open to sky cinema. It is located on Liwa Street (Previously Fatima Bint Mubarak Street) and (Publicly Al Najda street), near Kano Building. Though its location is almost very near to Al Maria Cinema and on the same street, I think it benefits from the surrounding hotels such as, Zakher, Al Hamra, Rotana, and many other hotels and crowds in the same area!.

Eldorado Cinema:

El Dorado Cinema, Zayed The First Street (Electra) ADOGD.

El Dorado Cinema, The First high-quality air-conditioned cinema in Abu Dhabi, was founded by its Lebanese owner Mr Atef Karam In 1970 by leasing Al Otaiba plot opposite to Omer Al Khayam (Now Al Hamra Hotel) for 30 years. The cinema was showing English and Malayalam films up to 1994, then Arabic films were introduced. El Dorado Cinema was shut down in 2017 after almost a half-century of pleasure and entertainment offered to Abu Dhabi city inhabitants. Thanks to, Mr Karam and thanks extended to Lebanese pioneers who began building cinemas and hotels in Abu Dhabi in earlier days, such as Emil Al Bustani of the Beach Hotel and the Late Albert Matta RIP, of Zakher Hotel, to attract tourists and businessmen to Abu Dhabi growing city.

Chapter 16: Abu Dhabi Top 5 Oldest Clubs

The Club:

The Club (Previously the British Club) has existed on the North East side of Abu Dhabi Island for 60 years. In 1958 the Petroleum Development (Trucial Coast) Ltd built a rest house (Majlis) for oilfield employees. The British Agent Hugh Boustead asked AD (TC) Ltd to give them the rest house as a club. In 1962 Sheikh Shakhbut RIP, Ruler of Abu Dhabi Emirate granted the rest house to the British Community. In 1967 Sheikh Zayed RIP, Ruler of Abu Dhabi Emirate granted The Club an extension to the seashore of Khor Bighal. The Club is now considered as the "oldest social club in Abu Dhabi".

The Rest house (British Club) 1958-1962

The Club as a non-profit social organisation has grown with Abu Dhabi city side by side. The members are multinational expats living in UAE. Some of them completed 40 years or more of membership. More than 50% of them are British Nationals.

In Abu Dhabi good old days, the club was a good place for the British "to defeat loneliness" and make delicious homemade food cooked and donated by active female members.

"The Club's frequently organizes beach parties. One day, the theme may be Asian culture. The other day any other culture from different parts of the world.

The bars and restaurants offer a wide variety of food. More than 50 different activities, ranging from fitness sports to sailing, diving, swimming, playing tennis, squash, football, snooker, hockey, etc., are available," *Qouted The Club"*.

The Club's Beach at sunset

The Club is the member's place to attain joyful life full of entertainment and fun in the moonlight or under the shining sun.

The Club's Beach

Al Emarat Sports Club:

(Previously, Al Ahli + Al Falah)

a)   Al Ahli Cultural and Sports Club:

Al Ahli Club Logo (Musabbah Al Mazroui)

Al Ahli Sports Club was established in Abu Dhabi in 1967 and is one of the oldest cultural and artistic sports clubs. Activities started within an old house next to Jashanmal's shop, located in the banking area. The club was moved into another house in the Power House community. With the scarcity of urbanisation and sports activity, the club moved to the headquarters of al-Wahda Club with its tremendous support.

The club's enthusiastic president, was Mohammed bin Abdul Jalil al-Fahim, when a group of youngmen met in al Al Qubaisi house behind Bin Sulayim's The club starred in its competitions and won the first league championship in 1969-1970 and the second in 1970-1971 house in early 1966. The delegation went to the diwan of His Highness Sheikh Shakhbut, who honoured them and agreed to their demand and suggested naming the (Ahli club) on them and the players to wear red and white, the colours of the flag of Abu Dhabi Emirate.

In 1967, Sheikh Hamdan bin Mohammed RIP gave them a popular empty land on Airport Street behind the Unity Mall. In 1969, the club was granted a large headquarters, al-Wahda Club today.

Al Ahli Club received Um Kulthoum, and many Syrian, Sudanese and Indian events.

In 1971 Sheikh Khalifa became honorary president of the club, and in 1973 a new board of directors was elected. In 1974, al-Ahli and Al Falah were merged under the name (Al Emarat Sports Club).

    b)   Al Falah Cultural and Sports Club:

Al Falah Sports Club Logo (Musabbah Al Mazroui)

In 1968, al-Falah Cultural Sports Club was founded in a public house of the Power House, Community, as one of the oldest cultural sports clubs.

The club's board of directors was formed in 1970 under the Department of Social Affairs and Labor supervision headed by Abdul Karim Abdullah Srour.

The distinguished players of Al-Falah Club were Mohammed Obeid, Fayrouz, Shamimel and Omar Youssef.

The Police Club:

Police Sports Cultural Club Logo (Musabbah Al Mazroui)

The Police Cultural Sports Club was established in 1967 and was based in one of the villas designed by consultant Medhat Mazloum to house government employees in Karama. He was founded by a senior police chief headed by Sheikh Mubarak bin Mohammed. The club's board of directors was formed by Vice President Hamad Bouka and featured many stars who won the cup of His Highness Sheikh Mubarak. His

Highness Sheikh Nahyan bin Mubarak became the honorary president of the Police Sports Cultural Club to succeed his late father, Sheikh Mubarak. Thus the police club opened its doors to the masses.

The club was granted land on the right of Arabian Gulf Street before the Section Bridge, where the luxury headquarters of the Police Officers Club was established, which features a large dome and a unique architectural design. A hotel currently occupies the site.

Abu Dhabi Sports Club:

(Previously, Al Ittihad + Al Wahda)

    c)   Al Itihad Cultural and Sports Club:

Al Itihad Club Logo (Musabbah Al Mazroui)

Al Itihad Cultural Sports Club was first established in hired house and then granted a public house at the Power House community, Abu Dhabi, in early 1969, by the Department of Social Affairs. An old cultural sports club headed by honorary president Sheikh Khadem Bin Buti, who provided financial assistance.

The club's first board of directors was formed in 1969 under the supervision of Khalifa Al-Qubaisi as president. The club was headed by an honorary chairmanship of Sheikh Hamdan Bin Mohammed in 1972. Sheikh Hamdan has made every care, and personal presence. Young men liked the name of Al Etihad Club at the time of union between the emirates.

Among the sports club football activities and their most important players were Amin, Fadlallah, Abu Eida and Osman al-Kabir.

d)	Al Wahda Cultural and Sports Club:

Al Wahda Sports Cultural Club Logo (Musabbah Al Mazroui)

He was founded in August 1969 in The Zaab region and then moved to a popular residence in the Al-Baorhos area headed by an honorary chairman of Sheikh Faisal bin Sultan al-Qasimi.

Among his players were Saleh Aidan, Massoud, Ahmed Hamed, Mohammed Ismail and others.

In 1974, the Itihad merged with Al Wahda Club under the name "**Abu Dhabi Sports Club**".

Tourist Club:

The Tourist Club Main Entrance

The Tourist Club and Beach was located next to Abu Dhabi Meridien Hotel. An interesting place to spend the weekend in Abu Dhabi. The Club had tennis courts, basketball, restaurants, pizzeria, snooker, gym and the bowling centre, mainly taking care of the Abu Dhabi Bowling Championship.

Abu Dhabi National Hotels Co. managed the Tourist Club before Compass Co. Sheikh Zayed used to visit the Club regularly with his visitors.

Sheikh Zayed RIP, used to play Bowling.

The Tourist club was affected by the road extension and demolished. Even the name of the area, which was referred to as (Tourist Club Area), was also changed to (Al Zahyah).

Chapter 17: Abu Dhabi Top 5 Old Hospitals

The Central Hospital:

The Central Hospital 1968

The site location of the Central Hospital was chosen according to the technical report of the directive plan of Abu Dhabi Town during the rule of Sheikh Shakhbout Bin Sultan, by Sir William Halcrow & Partners., and

Messrs. Scott Wilson /Kirkpatrick & Associates. In 26/2/1962. The central hospital was located in Sector West 13/01, within the then Khalifa Medical Services Complex, which is 55 acres.

The central hospital was built by the German company Ziebart, brokered by the Lebanese Victor Hashim and financed by Sheikh Shakhbout RIP, between 1964 and 1966. There had been an arbitration with the contractor, who had only supplied the hospital's ready-made caravans and failed to install the equipment because they were not included in the contract. The work remained suspended until Sheikh Zayed Bin Sultan took power in 1966 and solved the problem. It was opened in 1968 up to 2008.

Al Jazeera Hospital:

Al Jazeera Hospital 1980s

Health services in Abu Dhabi have witnessed remarkable development as the number of specialised workers has increased, and the therapeutic sector has seen an increment in the number of consultants, specialists, doctors, dentists, pharmacists, nurses and technicians, according to statistics from the Department of Planning and Economy in Abu Dhabi.

Al Jazeera Hospital, despite being provided by part of Khalifa Medical City, al-Jazeera is one of several hospitals including Zayed Al-Askari, Corniche Maternity, Mafraq and Emergency Hospital, Psychiatry, Physiotherapy Center, Dental Center, Zayed Herbal Medicine Center, Nursing Home, Al Rahba Hospital, Shakhbout Medical City, as well as maternity and childhood centres.

Al Jazeera Hospital was integrated into Khalifa Medical City, where the hospital's capacity was increased from 210 beds to 450 beds between 1999 and 2004 to keep pace with the development of the population, and for the first time added training rooms, continuing medical education and national campaigns for early detection of diseases within departments, institutions and commercial centres and to combat incurable diseases such as diabetes and hypertension. All this after the Health Services Authority of the Emirate of Abu Dhabi began operating the UAE's health facilities on a modern standards.

Khalifa Medical City W13/01

Corniche Hospital:

The Corniche maternity hospital 1978

In the sixteenth, there wasn't a specialized maternity hospital for giving birth. There was a small clinic besides Al Otaiba mosque, opposite to the British Agency, where my wife gave birth of our first baby daughter in 1970. Next year 1971 we got the second baby son in the central hospital.

Up to August 1977 women were giving birth in the central hospital and some were admitting Rashid Hospital in Dubai. Sheikh Zayed RIP instructed to convert Al Shaheen Hotel into Corniche Hospital. The original building of Shaheen Hotel was modified, though it was not suitable for a maternity hospital. Corniche Hospital was opened charging a fee of AED 50 per night, and changed to AED 200/night.

In the 1980s and 1990s the Corniche Hospital was the best maternity hospital in Abu Dhabi, provided with professional consultants, lady doctors, midwifes, and nurses. Some of the consultants like the Indian lady Dr John, Dr Harrison, Tom Buchanan, Dr Al Sheikh, Rob Elliot, Tony Alexander, and many more. In 1994 there were employees of 72 nationalities working in.

Corniche Maternity Hospital, Abu Dhabi Corniche 2021

The New Corniche Maternity Hospital with its view, adjacent to Abu Dhabi Sheraton Hotel, is one of the best maternity hospitals in UAE.

Mafraq Hospital:

Mafraq Hospital with Royal Wings

Mafraq Hospital was one of the oldest hospitals outside Abu Dhabi Island, opened in 1983. It was a referral treatment hospital with 451 beds. Services include paediatrics, medicine, obstetrics, as well as surgery and acute care services.

Mafraq Hospital was a leading trauma centre and operated the critical burn unit owned by Abu Dhabi Health Services Company PJSC (SEHA).

The Doctors are internationally recognised, accredited and experienced. Services and stuff shifted to Sheikh Shakhbout Medical City constructed to the nearby vicinity.

The new facility serves as the community hospital for one of the fastest-growing areas in the Emirate of Abu Dhabi, as per Abu Dhabi Vision 2030.

Zayed Military Hospital:

Zayed Military Hospital, Arabian Gulf Street

Zayed Military Hospital is at the forefront of medical institutions in providing medical care to military patients and their families, civilian citizens and residents. It was opened in October 1979 as "Zayed Military Hospital."

The beginning was in 1966 in a small clinic in Al Nahyan Camp, where the Abu Dhabi Defense Force was later transformed into a field hospital in Al-Falah camp.

The year 1979, was considered the beginning of medical services, where four field units were formed by 1980, and in 1983 the mobile field surgery unit was formed. In 1986 the School of Medical Services was received to contribute to the rehabilitation of auxiliary medical personnel from technicians and nurses.

Zayed Military Hospital is one of the oldest hospitals in Abu Dhabi, started with Abu Dhabi Defence Force clinic at Al Nahyan Camp.

Chapter 18: Abu Dhabi Top 5 Oldest Cemeteries

Al Bateen Cemetery:

New Bateen Cemetery, Arabian Gulf Street, Abu Dhabi

Al Bateen Cemetery lies at Al Bateen area, between Al Khaleej Al Arabi Street East and Al Bateen Street West. Hazza Bin Zayed Street

South and Al Ghadeer Street North. It is one of the oldest cemeteries on Abu Dhabi Island.

Zayed Bin Khalifa Bin Shakhbut Bin Dhiab Bin Eisa Al Nahyan (1837-1909) Zayed Al Kabeer, the seventh ruler in the necklace of al-Nahyan's rulers, rests in Peace. He was the great leader of the Abu Dhabi Emirate, the grandfather of His Highness Sheikh Zayed Bin Sultan Al-Nahyan, the founder of the United Arab Emirates in 1971. Also, it includes the grave of Sheikha Mariam Bint Sultan RIP, the sister of H.H Sheikh Zayed Bin Sultan RIP.

Al Bateen Cemetery was updated as a historical cemetery and the area around it was developed as high-quality residential buildings.

Al Dana 3 Cemetery:

Al Dana 3 Cemetery, Liwa Street, Abu Dhabi

One of the oldest cemeteries in sector E9, along Liwa Street (Previously Fatima Bint Mubarak Street), to the northside of Al Maria Cinema and Mall. Only a few graves exist inside the wide compound. A big part of it where no graves was cut and converted into Mawaqif public parking for the adjacent high rise building towers.

Zayed City Cemetery 1:

It is located in sector E4/01 Abu Dhabi. A Six-sided compound, east side of Rashid Bin Saeed Street (formerly Airport Street), opposite Al Manhal Palace. One of the oldest cemeteries in Abu Dhabi Island. Burial was postponed a long time ago when Mahwi Cemetery on Al Ain Road was opened. Al-Fatih Mosque is located on the North Western corner of the cemetery, and to the East of it lies the Private Jubilee International School.

Another cemetery (Zayed City Cemetery 2) is located in the same Sector on Zayed The First Street besides NMC Hospital, where few graves exist.

Corniche Cemetery:

Corniche Cemetery

An old cemetery has existed besides Al Corniche Maternity Hospital for long. Few graves have been there for decades, and burial was postponed. Recently, the cemetery was maintained and named as Corniche Cemetery (Maqbarat Al Corniche).

<u>Um Al Nar (Sas Al Nakhl Non Muslim Cemetry):</u>

Um Al Nar (Sas Al Nakhl Non Muslim Cemetry)

The presence of Christian cemeteries in the UAE, in general, is due to the presence of a large number of foreign Christian residents. Of course, they are Arabs, Asians, European and other nationals.

The first church was built in Abu Dhabi city on the land granted by the Ruler of Abu Dhabi in 1963, preceded by the construction of a church in Sir Bani Yas, where the island was used as an airstrip for landing and transit base in 1935. Even Christian followers of the Nestorian Doctrine lived on that Island before Islam Faith overwhelmed the Arab Peninsula and the coasts of the Gulf.

Um Al Nar (Sas Al Nakhl Non Muslim Cemetery)

Abu Dhabi's oldest Christian cemetery has also been designated in the Sas al-Nakhl area, outside Al-Maqta Bridge. It was surrounded by roads and bridges on each side.

Abu Dhabi Municipality Health section has managed the cemetery since its inception in the 1960s. The cemeteries had accurate records under the supervision of inspectors of the municipal health section.

New cemeteries were allocated at Bani Yas area for Muslims and Christians, indicating tolerance and that God the Greatest is One.

Chapter 19: Abu Dhabi Top 5 Oldest Parks

Al Khalidiya Park:

Al Khalidiya Park, Zayed The First Street

His Highness Sheikh Zayed bin Sultan RIP has sought from the outset to spread the green colour in the country, saying, "Give me agriculture, I give you civilisation."

Abu Dhabi town planning considered the construction of parks and landscaping agriculture along streets, squares and intersections. The municipality established the Khalidiya nursery and the Al-Manhal nursery. Abu Dhabi has become a city of magic as beautiful as Al Khalidiya Park on Arabian Gulf and Zayed I streets. It occupies 65,000 square meters and is the first park to be made in Abu Dhabi in 1974. In the middle are a large water fountain and two smaller manaforts. The garden has been fenced with concrete bricks removed lately. It has footpaths and wooden seats.

Al Asima Park:

Asima Park Site Before Execution

The site of Al Asima Park (Abu Dhabi's Capital Garden) between the early 1960s and the early 1970s. All houses of wood, tents and palm fronds were removed. Only palm trees and other shrubs remained in the early 1970s, as a prelude to constructing

The houses that occupied the site in the 1960s were transformed into a beautiful gardens surrounded by walls in the 1970s. Now all the walls are removed and all gardens open to view by the public by decision of the higher authorities now.

Al Asima Park (Capital Garden), location was chosen by H.H Sheikh Zayed RIP and executed after the construction of al-Khalidiya Park.

*Al Asima Park, Khalifa Bin Zayed The First Stre*et in the 1990s

Family Park:

Family Park, Abu Dhabi Corniche

This area, which was randomly consisted of palm fronds cottages in the past, has become a public park called "Family Park", one of the most wonderful parks in Abu Dhabi liked by local inhabitants and tourists. It is in a privileged location of downtown along the Corniche of Abu Dhabi, where it is easy to reach the beach in front and enjoy beautiful landscapes, colourful fountains, and decorated shrubs. Together with many facilities for children playings, shaded areas to sit and relax along with a lot of open green spaces and a variety of places dedicated to playing volleyball, tennis and basketball with the presence of cycling corridors and barbecue areas.

Old Airport Park:

Old Airport Park, Rashid Bin Saeed Street

Al Bateen Airport Garden (Wimpy) is one of the oldest gardens on both sides of Airport Street. We used to stroll through this children's play park with an Abu Dhabi cafeteria opened by Kuwait Food Company (Americana) in the vicinity of the sports city in the early 1970s.

The Abu Dhabi Municipality's cafeteria building has been upgraded topped with a KFC badge on Al Mashjar Street, which is located on Rashid Bin Saeed Street (formerly Airport Street) and the main entrance to Zayed Sports City opposite the Hilton Abu Dhabi hotel, as well as many branches within Abu Dhabi and its environs!

Um Al Emarat Park:

Um Al Emarat Park, Al Karama Street

It's located on the opposite side of Al Mushref Palace in Sector W24/01 along Al Karma Street to the west of the International School of Chouefat.

Um Al Emarat Park was upgraded to be one of the largest and oldest parks in Abu Dhabi. It was called Al Mushrif Park and constructed for women and kids only. Its renovation made it an amazing family park in Abu Dhabi.

Extensive facilities were introduced, including the Great Lawn, Animal Barn operated with Emirates Park Zoo, including camels, sheep and goats, cows.

The Amphitheatre is such a large place to perform arts, Botanic Garden, Children's Garden and Evening Garden.

Chapter 20: Top 5 Demolished But Still Remembered

Old Custom House:

Old Custom House, Corniche Road

Abu Dhabi custom building was on the Corniche to the east of Abu Dhabi Municipality Building. It was facing the seashore and the small jetty (Al-Fardha). Duty fees were imposed by the Department of Customs on goods piled in the storage yard. The building was built when Indian

Traders used to land in Abu Dhabi to meet Abu Dhabi traders of Pearls. The building looks like an old customs building of Bombay Mughal architecture, inspired during the British Mandate of India. It was an amazing landmark brutally removed in the late 60s. This building "Custom House", was called publically "Bombay Building" for the reasons mentioned above.

The Custom's offices were occupying the ground floor. It was mentioned that the building was built by the well known Pearl trader Khalf bin Abdullah Bin Otaiba RIP, who built the near by mosque on the corniche in 1930s.

(*Info Mustafa Alhendi*)

Clock Tower:

Clock Tower, Abu Dhabi Corniche

The clock tower was in the centre of the oval roundabout on the corniche. To the west of it was Al-Otaibat Mosque amid the trees and greenery. They were demolished but still remembered. We hope that they can be rebuilt on the same ground after the Corniche widening is especially finished!

Volcano Fountain:

Volcano Fountain, Abu Dhabi Corniche (ADOGD)

Volcano Fountain is a Symbolic structure consisting of six horizontal platform levels and six vertical stepped passages from bottom to top. It resembles the 6 Gulf Arab Countries (GCC) Cooperation. A symbolic icon designed by Abu Dhabi Municipal Engineer Mr Alfi Girgis, constructed in 1988 and brutally demolished in 2004.

Volcano Fountain, Abu Dhabi Corniche under demolition (Paul Woodlock)

GCC Fountain:

*GCC Fountain, Baynouna Street (*Fountain of Cooperation was on Baynouna Street (now King Abdullah Bin Abdulaziz Al Saud Street), in front of the Intercontinental Hotel Abu Dhabi, symbolises the cooperation of the Gulf Arab states. Built on the occasion, the GCC Rulers held their second summit in Abu Dhabi in 1986.

The fountain was affected by the development of Baynouna Street widening and the introduction of light signals!

Al Hosn Mosque:

*The Stunning Mosque was built at the corner of Qasr Al Hosn in 1988,
with its circular dome, on Hamdan Bin Mohammed Street*

Al Hosn Palace

The mosque demolished as part of Al Hosn Palace renovation project.

Mr. Paul Woodlock, an active Historian and admin of Abu Dhabi Old Good Days Group says:

"I've nothing against development, improvements and a bit of expansion, but demolishing everything that's over 20 years old means the city will never develop a soul or a personality.

For example, the corniche could have quickly been developed and improved without demolishing the Volcano Fountain or the lovely oyster fountain. Or even more, sadly, the old customs house, which dates back to at least the 1930s and an iconic centrepiece of the corniche, could have been kept but sadly was simply torn down in the early 1970s. Even Al-Hosn fort isn't original now, but mostly a reconstruction."

Chapter 21: Author's Top 5 Artwork Designs

UAE University Logo:

UAE University Logo Design 1974

I was lucky to design the United Arab Emirates University logo and won the first prize in 1974. I was honoured by the late, His Excellency Khalfan Al Roumi, undersecretary of the Ministry of Education at that time. The curve of the prize of ten thousand dirhams was rewarding then.

United Arab Emirates University was founded in 1976. Since then I am proud of participating in the logo design competition and winning the first prize.

UAE 15th National Day Stamp Design:

Al Jazeera Club Logo Design:

In 1982, I had the privilege of winning the design of the logo of Al Jazeera Sports Club in Abu Dhabi. The first thing that came to my mind when I played daily maps and plans of Abu Dhabi Island, as responsible for the drawing and artistic archive unit of the Department of City Planning, but I put the map of Abu Dhabi Island (Outline) in the centre of the logo to say: Abu Dhabi city Dora al-Madain starts from the flame of liberation and union, and meets its youth in sports stadiums to compete honourably, to be the shield of the homeland. The committee well received the design, and

I was awarded the first prize with a cash value of 3,000 dirhams. In black and white, a striped background was later placed to show the logo more clearly on the players' shirts and badges.

UNICEF Stamp Designs

One million Stamps on child growth.

The General Postal Authority (GPA) issued 1 million stamps to commemorate UNICEF, the United Nation Children Fund) child survival and development revolution.

The issue had form denomination dipecting different themes important in child growth and development: AED 2 (Breast feeding), AED 1.75 (Oral rehydration), AED 1 (Immunization Therapy), and AED 50 fills (Growth Monitory).

The predominant colours in the four stamps all carrying the UNICEF's Logo are blue and green pastels.

The stamps designed by Assad El Abba, an artist at Unicef's and Town Planning Department offices.

Safe Energy Stamps:
Half Million Stamps on Energy Conservation

The General Postal Authority issued a set of two stamps on Energy Conservation.

The stamps of the demonstration of AED 2 and 50 Fills. The GPA had advertised in the local papers in iting the public to send their designs on the "Save Energy" Concept.

The winning designs submitted by Assad El Abbas adorn the stamps and are colourful and symbolic, emphasizing various energy sources with related concept-Solar power, oil and water etc.

The stamps in the standard form sizes of 30mm×40mm. The printer Cartor and France, has received a print order of 25,000 in each denomination.

Chapter 22: Miscellaneous

Cloth Washing (Dhobi Ghat):

Cloth Drying (<u>Dhobi Ghat</u>)

In the 1960s, we were amazed by the Indians' way of washing clothes. The Indians used to put our clothes in basins full of water and trampled them with their legs; then they were striking beating them on the wooden columns they erected intending to get rid of the water. Finally, spreading them on the sandy earth to dry and take rest according to the professional's rules. We used to receive our shirts with buttons smashed and fortunately ironed by the charcoal iron.

Lilam:

Typical Lilam Carrying Cloth Bags (Itihad Newspaper)

Lilam was walking around all day with a bag of clothes, toys and children's shoes, selling them to women customers fond of buying all that cheap, though knowing that the goods are of the low brand.

Ever since he entered the neighbourhood, he's been yelling: "Lilam. Oh, Lilam. Cheap it's cheap." So the women have gathered around on the floor lobby to find out what was new with him.

Lilam was a mobile shop without a license from the municipality.

Lilam has become rare to see after being popular in selling cheap goods. The job was left for the home delivery a few years later!

Old Taxi Service:

Old Gold and White Taxi in Abu Dhabi

Taxis had operated in white and gold since the beginning. The taxi drivers were very poor and worked hard day and night to earn money. The taxi rate was AED 2 and the taxi driver's earning was very less. He usually sleeps inside his taxi because he sends his income to his family he can't pay for a room. The taxi drivers were cooperative and each one pays AED 10 per month as an insurance gatherings in case of deadly accidents. The fund was paid as Diyya if any taxi caused death.

In accordance with Article 3 of Law No. 19 of 2006, the old taxis were scheduled to disappear from the streets of Abu Dhabi by the end of 2012 and be replaced by new taxis of the "silver" colour, under the time plan set by the Taxi Regulatory Center.

Abu Dhabi has retired from old taxis, after nearly three decades of service in white and gold, and introduced new taxis since 2008 to meet public transport requirements and conform to the development of the capital.

The new system included advanced technologies such as air navigation systems and digital maps, as well as service communication systems, smart data preservation systems and wireless communication with the customer service centre.

Randomly 80s-90s Shop Names:

The variety of shops in the 1980s and 1990s in Abu Dhabi

<u>**Sample Shop Names**</u>

Sana Stores/ Boutique Bent 20 / Ghazal Boutique / Marketing and Saving / Adam & Eve / Splash / Rotana / BHS / Ahlia Brzonic/ Dana Plaza / Dunya Al-Ajayeb / Al Kamal Bakery / Arlycan Sweets / Lebanese Toaster / Dairy Queen / Take and Save / Cooperative Society / IBrahimi / Zahrat Lebanon / Shaheen / Jashinmal / Penderosa Restaurant / Al Salam Stores / Perfection / Paul Jordan / Abu Azzouz / Saeed Bin Makhashen / Salmeen / Hamed Center / Hamdan Center / 1 Dirham Plaza / Green House / Maroush Modern Bakery / Al Saadah Bakery / Al Falah Plaza / Ambassador / Emsons / Sea side / Smoking Center /Lamsi/Gulf Plaza/Ambassador Style/Lacaza Café/Abella/Cheese and Pickles/Lebanese Loaf/United Color of Benetton/LaBrioch Café/Al Kamal Bakery/Sinfabad Electronic Games/Alamein/Al Rayyan/Gulf Bakery/Naeem Sweets/Samadi Sweets/Panache Chocolate/UAE Markets/Quick Savings/ Farmer Plaza/Dada Bay/Cheese Center/Abu Alwaleed/Arya/Khanji Laqshe/Fish Hut/KM/Arkan/Samadi/Safadi/Lulu Center/Marks & Spencer/Golden Fork/Tent Bakery/ Al Khayam Shawarma / Bouquet for Fabrics / Jewelry Access / Ayoub For Children's Clothing / Boutique Aria / Abu Dhabi Cooperative Society/ Al Fawzan Shops / Madinat Zayed Shopping Center / Egyptian Products / Old Market /Corniche Bakeries / Sultan Bakeries / Hamdan Center / Hamed Center / Port Market / Chicken Tikka / Abu Shakra / Kids / Panash / Bakery Algeria / Palestine Bakery / Golden Crown / Quick Saving Center / Mansour Sweets / Al Kamal Restaurant / Restaurant Al Sofon/ Abu Tafish/ Baby Shop / Zahrat Lebanon / Maroush / Oyster Sea / Ambassador

Style / Lakshmi / Fatima Supermarket / Levco / Alula Pharmacy / Posters / Green Branch / Junior / Fayyad / BHS / Marks & Spencer / Dana Plaza / Central Market / Juma Al Majid / Abu Kabi Grills / Al-Oberg/Mandarin Chinese/Golden fish/Sena Chopra/Al-Muhairi Center/Shuetram/Sadaf/Fatima Supermarket / Gift Friend / Honduras / French Cottage/ Golden Fork / Peace Shops / Al Jamal / Abeer Shops / Blue Marine / Albert Abella / Grey McKenzie / Chic Bibi / Katya / Khanji Shops / Jarir Library / Istanbul / Ard al Marsh/ World of Joy / Emirates General Market / University Library / Cafeteria Sunin /Issam/Thomason Library/Shaheen Supermarket/Emirates Discount Market/Old Zakhar/Tourist Club/New Market/ AED Plaza / Star of the Sea / Green House / Shell / UAE Markets / Lulu / Coral / Falcon Nest / Malik and Shaheed/ Cairo Fabrics / Sayed Kamal / Sheikha Fabrics / Abu Alwaleed / Children's Shop / Dana Plaza / Golden Fish Restaurant / Smoking Center / Cheese Center / Ya Mal Al Sham / Paint Restaurant / Egyptian Products / Sweidan / Krashi / British Fashion House / Al Alamein Cafeteria/ Al Umara Restaurant/ Wimpy / Rainbow Restaurant / Fatatari Hussein / Golden Bakery / Sweet Home / Printing Company / Automatic Grills / Habari House / Baalbek Hotel / Damascus Restaurant / Playboy / Black Cat / Yateem Glasses / Maher Supermarket / Abu Dhabi Mall / Marina Mall /Gallerya Mall/ Naeem Sweets/ Al Saeed Bakery/ She Zone Center.

Chapter 23: Questionnaire

Q&A

This questionnaire was asked to the author about his impression as an eyewitness on Abu Dhabi Town Planning Development during the last 5 decades.

Abu Dhabi General View from East to West

Question 1: What were your first impressions of Abu Dhabi when you arrived?

Answer: Arriving in Abu Dhabi in 1968 has a passion. I arrived on the Heron aircraft landed on the airstrip, on Abu Dhabi mid-island, from Bahrain. When I got off the aircraft, it was too hot. There was a temporary building with an immigration desk, where I received all the warm welcome.

My municipal driver of the double gear Landrover moved on the sandy track in the desert. When we reached the so far Guesthouse (Al Madheef) and did not find a vacant room to rest, I said to myself better to go back home.

The driver told me it was challenging to find a room in Abu Zabi. He moved to the old Municipality building on the Corniche beside the Custom-house. I was welcomed by Mr Tajuddine Al-Qadi, who thankfully invited me to be his roommate. Water was rare, and drinking water was more expensive than cigarettes. It was the most favourite gift for the guest.

Abu Dhabi was a small town consisting of a few rows of stone buildings on the beach. Partial demolishing of the city centre, and scattered new buildings on Hamdan and khalifa streets. Other wooden houses were temporary and made of palm fronds with cloth burjeels at the top.

Question 2: Can you talk about your journey to get to Abu Dhabi - where were you before? How did you hear about Abu Dhabi, and why did you come here?

Answer: I arrived in Abu Dhabi at the age of 24, specifically on 13/2/1968 from Beirut via Bahrain. After waiting one hour or so boarded to Abu Dhabi on a small Heron aircraft of Gulf Air. Abu Dhabi airstrip was enough for small Dakota and Heron aircraft.

I studied architectural draughtsmanship and building construction at the UN Training Centre in Damascus and finished my studies with distinction. The reason I was nominated for a scholarship for further studies in Sweden. I got the opportunity to work in the Planning Section of Abu Dhabi Municipality on an external contract basis offered by Mr Takahashi, Abu Dhabi Chief Town Planner. In 1969, I enrolled in a remote study programme in International Schools, London, and got my Architecture Diploma in 1973. Since then, I have been in the UAE.

During my employment, I attended GIS courses sponsored by Stratford University UK, in conjunction with the Norwegian Norplan Consultant and Gulf computers. I lived here for almost 54 years and have good relations with my fellow citizens and expatriates. I retired in 2012 as an Information Expert of Spatial Data Directorate, Town Planning Sector.

Question 3: What were the biggest challenges in the urban planning of Abu Dhabi?

Answer: The Long Sighted Sheikh Zayed RIP ordered Arabicon to Revise the Master Plan done by Halcrow. H.H insisted that all roads should be straight (Seda).

The biggest challenge in urban planning was to fulfil the urgent needs of inhabitants, especially the main infrastructure projects already designated in 1962:

- The Airport, to connect Abu Dhabi with the external world
- Al-Maqta Bridge, to connect Abu Dhabi with the mainland.
- Al Mina (Harbour), to import and export goods
- Central Hospital to treat the patients and women's birth delivery.
- The power station and desalination plant, to get electricity and water.
- Abu Dhabi Defense Force Headquarters, to secure the country.
- Sewerage Plant to dispose
- Abu Dhabi Zoo and take care of animals (camels, horses, cows and goats)
- Dredging and Reclamation to reduce the seawater level.
- Modification of the plan to be a grid network.
- Building Abu Dhabi- Al Ain Road.

Question 4: What was it like to work with Dr Makhlouf?

Answer: In 1968, Dr Abdulrahman Makhlouf, the UN Town Planning expert, was nominated by the Ruler H.H. Sheikh Zayed Bin Sultan Al Nahyan. He put down a marvellous master plan for Abu Dhabi Island. CBD was designed, Land use and building heights were defined.

Dr Makhlouf founded Town Planning Department as an independent governmental authority to plan, supervise, and follow up constructions and building permits of the Abu Dhabi Emirate. We used to work hard day and night as a team and members of one family. Together with my colleagues, we spent a lot of time apart from our newly married wives to submit our plans and representations to the Ruler after midnight. HH Sheikh Zayed was awakened and slept very little. Dr Makhlouf's spirit and feelings were totally embedded in Abu Dhabi Town and its road network as we consider Abu Dhabi as our beloved homeland.

Question 5: What do you see when you look at Abu Dhabi City now? Are you proud of what you helped create?

Answer: Abu Dhabi witnessed a huge urban development. One of the most prominent features was the skyscrapers that arose in the city centre and high frise buildings in the tourist club area (Al Zahia).

As a result, they grew up dramatically. When I walk amid the streets, I feel lost. Undoubtedly, the movement of vertical architectural investment in the CBD was dictated by the most necessities: 1. The area available for the development is geographically limited. 2. High population density due to the open door policy and large commercial and financial activities. 3. The difference in customs and traditions between the UAE citizens and the expatriates.

Nevertheless, the vertical development required appropriate solutions in traffic and parking spaces. Living areas lack ventilation and light. Moreover, the architectural models used, consisting of aluminum and glass cladding, raised the dwelling temperature in such a way the use of air conditioners has been significantly continuous for most months of the year, in the absence of natural ventilation.

Abu Dhabi changed its Islamic cover and wore a blue coloured transparent stretch. No more Architecture. Everything locks typically commercial.

Question 6: Can you talk about Sheikh Zayed's input into City planning and architecture? What was it like to bring his vision to life?

Answer: Cities like individuals have a specific date of birth. H.H managed the UAE political transformation together with the construction of Abu Dhabi to be the capital city, using his long experience in Al-Ain as the Ruler's representative (1946-1966)

Frankly speaking, Sheikh Zayed was the real Town Planner, the Supervisor, the Landlord, and the Gardener. He used to carry his stick as a drawing instrument. He marked his vision and planned on the sand. With his stick, Zayed has drawn the finest lines and pointed to the perfect project locations. Lines turned into Roads, roundabouts, and maps turned into schools, hospitals, police stations, mosques, etc.

Question 7: What we some of the logos and brands you helped create (Stamp design, for example)?

Answer: Depending on my UK study in Commercial Art, I was lucky to participate in Logo and stamp design competitions:

•I am proud to be the designer of the UAE University Logo in 1974.

•It was a great pleasure to celebrate 'World Earth Hour' that took place globally on March 30, from (8:30 pm to 9:30 pm). By joining this global event by designing Save Energy Stamps, 1997, we ensure our commitment towards saving energy and providing it for others in need.

•Logo Designer of Al Jazeera Club.

•Logo Designer of UAE Olympic Committee.

Question 8: Can you describe those early years of the UAE when so much was being built and created? What was it like bringing so many new things to life?

Answer: In the 1970s, Abu Dhabi witnessed a rapid construction movement in various areas, mainly commercial buildings with specific heights up to 7 floors with unit air conditioning. Flats were available and comfortable. In 1981, Khalifa Committee was entrusted technically, financially, and legally to supervise the commercial buildings in Abu Dhabi to achieve urban and economic development. It was also entrusted with selecting consultants, contracting them, bidding and signing contracts, and following up the implementation of contractors' and consultants' contracts until delivery.

Demolition and construction were active in the 1990s, and centrally air-conditioned highrise towers with residents' parking spaces below grew up.

Flats became more comfortable and vacant to choose the best. The residents' extended stay was assured, and the building constructions showed pleasant interiors and exteriors.

Question 9: Do you have any favourite buildings or locations in Abu Dhabi City?

Answer: Favourite buildings in Abu Dhabi are numerous. The most important among these still standing:

- Qasr Al Hisn with its magnificent architecture and heritage.
- Zayed Bin Sultan Mosque, by Architect Joseph Abdulki.
- Cultural Foundation by the well known Uk John Harris

- Al Kalily Building Zayed the First street by the Egyptian Dr Farouk Al Johari

- Al Otaiba 5 storey Building, Hamdan Street by the Egyptian Dr Jalal Momen.

- Al Omeira building, Hamdan Street, by the Egyptian Dr Farouk Al Johari.

- Al Mushref Palace by the Egyptian Dr Kurayem.

- Coconut (Al Bahr) Twin Towers.

- Emirates Palace, Corniche Road.

- Qasr Al Watan, Al Ras Al Akhder.

- Khalifa Bin Zayed the First Mosque. Al Hisn Street by the Egyptian Dr Dawood Al Rajhi.

Question 10: What were some of the key considerations early in the planning process for Abu Dhabi City?

Answer: His Highness Sheikh Zayed RIP has drawn up the outlines of planning. Key considerations were in mind:

- The streets should be straight.

- To preserve palm trees, locating gardens, planting roadsides, central road Islands, roundabouts with fountains, trees, herbs and flowers.

- Preserve the Arab-Islamic heritage in planning and construction.

- Lower the underground water level of Abu Dhabi Island by dredging and reclamation and expanding the island's area by sand filling.

- Fix the building heights and number of floors for each sector according to land use.

- UAE citizens deserve 4 types of lands (Residential, commercial, industrial, and farm).

- Gardens and parks, open areas for families and future extension.

- Clean beaches for both males and females.

- Green belts along the highway to stop sandy storms.

- Electric current, street lighting, water supply, drainage, and garbage collection etc.

First Row Right to Left: Late Thani Bin Murshid, Dr. Makhlouf, and Myself

Question 11: Can you explain the differences between the different Urban Planners, specifically Takahashi and Makhlouf?

Answer: Mr Takahashi RIP studied Architecture and Town Planning at Columbia University in New York in the 60s. I used to accompany him, to present the general and detailed plans to the Crown Prince Diwan in Al Ain. Takahashi RIP was a pragmatical man proud of his academic qualifications and knowledge. He was therefore proposing what he sees fit without offering alternatives. He was relying on his academic qualifications without giving a written formal explanation in Arabic. So it was difficult to understand his proposals in the absence of alternatives.

On the other side, Sheikh Zayed welcomed Dr Makhlouf as manager of Abu Dhabi Emirate Town Planner. His Arabic language was easy to understand. Zayed had expressed his desire to lay down the key rules of Islamic architecture in the UAE by exchanging ideas and proposals instead of plans based on academic qualifications.

In an outdoor interview, Sheikh Zayed asked Dr Makhlouf: "What do you want to offer for us? Shall you tell us here are the drawings? Please carry it out without hearing what we want."

Dr Makhlouf listened for a while and said, "Your Highness, we'll propose several solutions as alternatives, and your Highness chose the most appropriate to your needs." Sheikh Zayed was happy and said to him: "Go ahead, God blessing!"

CONGRATULATIONS!!

Happy Golden Jubilee on the occasion of UAE 50th National Day!!

About The Author

The author Assad Houssein El Abbas (55 Years Eyewitness)

Born in 1945 at Fassouta, Palestine. He has been living in Abu Dhabi, United Arab Emirates, for more than five decades, since 13th February 1968. He went to UN Primary and Intermediate schools in Lebanon. He finished secondary studying at Al Etihad Secondary School Tyre, Lebanon. Then joined three years Diploma course in Architecture and Building Construction at UN Institute in Damascus. He got the first outstanding among his classmates and was entitled to a scholarship for one year for further studies in Sweden in 1967. He completed his four-years BA in Architecture from International Schools London in 1973, together with three years Diploma in Commercial Art, from Sheffield College UK.

Since his childhood, he was fond of drawing geometrical shapes, getting mature, he was fond of Town Planning and Architecture.

In 1968, El Abbas joined Abu Dhabi Town Planning Section, Abu Dhabi Municipally. At that time, Arabicon had already revised the Abu Dhabi master plan done by Messers Halcrow / Scot Wilson KerkPatrek, supervised by the Late Japanese architect, Dr Katsuhiko Takahashi, Abu Dhabi Chief Town Planner. Later, he was appointed as head of the Drawing Unit of the planning section, Abu Dhabi Town Planning Department, managed by Dr. Abdulrahman Makhlouf. A few years later, in the 1990s, he attended advanced GIS (Geographic Information Systems) courses managed by Stratford University, sponsored by the Norwegian Consultants Norplan. El Abbas was chosen to supervise the Urban Planning Digital Data collected by Gulf Computers, related to Injazat LMS (Land Management System) pilot project for Abu Dhabi Municipality and Town Planning Sector. Two years later, in March 2009, Mr. El Abbas was appointed as GIS (Geographical Information System) Expert at Abu Dhabi Spatial Data Directorate until his retirement in 2012.

Book References

1. Lectures by Dr. Abdulrahman Makhlouf, Director of the Department of Town Planning (1968-1976)

2. Rehlat Al Omr Ma Al Omran Book, Half a Century in Urbanization Dr Abdulrahman Makhlouf (1968-2014)

3. Abu Dhabi Statistical Yearbook- Abu Dhabi Emirate

4. Encyclopedia of Legislation / Part II Secretariat of the Executive Council

5. Dr. Alamira Reem Bani Hashim, Planning Abu Dhabi/ An Urban History Book.

6. Historical Studies/ Fatima Al Mansoori, Director of Zayed Center for Studies and Research, Emirates. Heritage Club.

7. Archives of the Town Planning Department, Abu Dhabi Municipality.

8. Halcrow/Scott Wilson Kirk Patrick & partners Report 1962 in English.

9. Department of Municipalities and Agriculture - Al Asima Magazine - Abu Dhabi Municipality.

10. Al Bayan Printing and Publishing Foundation - Al Bayan Newspaper – Dubai

11. Emirates Media Corporation - Al Ittihad Newspaper - Abu Dhabi.

12. The National Newspaper English

13. Statistics issued by the Department of Planning and Coordination - Abu Dhabi.

14. Dr. Mohammed al-Qudsi, Book "Zayed…Omer The Third",

15. The Late Eng. Kamal Hamza, Manager Dubai Municipality 1960s.

16. Dr. Khalil Ailabouni, Book "The Beginnings".

17. Musabah Al Mazruei Book: (Abu Dhabi

18. Football, Start and Foundation).

19. Abu Dhabi Good Old Days Group.

20. Mr. Paul Woodlock (Abu Dhabi & Dubai Blogs Admin).

21. The author's blogs and writings as an eyewitness.

* 9 7 8 1 9 1 5 4 2 4 3 9 6 *